M000237774

To the Reader:

Scientology® applied religious philosophy contains pastoral counseling procedures intended to assist an individual to gain greater knowledge of self. The mission of the Church of Scientology is a simple one: to help the individual achieve greater self-confidence and personal integrity, thereby enabling him to really trust and respect himself and his fellow man. The attainment of the benefits and goals of Scientology philosophy requires each individual's dedicated participation, as only through his own efforts can he achieve these.

This book is based on the religious literature and works of the Scientology Founder, L. Ron Hubbard. It is presented to the reader as part of the record of his personal research into life, and the application of same by others, and should be construed only as a written report of such research and not as a statement of claims made by the Church or the Founder.

Scientology philosophy and its forerunner, Dianetics® spiritual healing technology, as practiced by the Church, address only the "thetan" (spirit). Although the Church, as are all churches, is free to engage in spiritual healing, it does not, as its primary goal is increased spiritual awareness *for all. For this reason, the Church does not wish to accept individuals who desire treatment of physical or mental illness but prefers to refer these to qualified specialists of other organizations who deal in these matters.*

The Hubbard® Electrometer is a religious artifact in the Church Confessional. It in itself does nothing, and is used by ministers only to assist parishioners in locating areas of spiritual distress or travail.

We hope the reading of this book is only the first stage of a personal voyage of discovery into this new and vital world religion.

Church of Scientology International

This book belongs to:

_____

_____

(Date)

SCIENTOLOGY 0-8
The Book of Basics

L. RON HUBBARD

SCIENTOLOGY 0-8
The Book of Basics

Bridge
PUBLICATIONS, INC.

Published in the U.S.A. by
Bridge Publications, Inc.
4751 Fountain Avenue
Los Angeles, California 90029

ISBN 0-88404-376-2

Published in other countries by
New Era® Publications International, ApS
Store Kongensgade 55
1264 Copenhagen K, Denmark

ISBN 87-7336-573-4

Copyright © 1988 L. Ron Hubbard Library
ALL RIGHTS RESERVED

Second Printing 1989

Scientology, Dianetics, Hubbard, E-Meter, Celebrity Centre, Flag,
Scientology cross and *Scientologist* are trademarks and service marks
owned by Religious Technology Center and used with its permission.

No part of this book may be reproduced or utilized in any form or by
any means electronic or mechanical, including photocopying, recording
or by any information storage and retrieval system, without
the permission of the copyright owner.

Printed in the United States of America

Important Note

In reading this book, be very certain you never go past a word you do not fully understand.

The only reason a person gives up a study or becomes confused or unable to learn is because he or she has gone past a word that was not understood.

The confusion or inability to grasp or learn comes AFTER a word that the person did not have defined and understood.

Have you ever had the experience of coming to the end of a page and realizing you didn't know what you had read? Well, somewhere earlier on that page you went past a word that you had no definition for or an incorrect definition for.

Here's an example. "It was found that when the crepuscule arrived the children were quieter and when it was not present, they were much livelier." You see what happens. You think you don't understand the whole idea, but the inability to understand came entirely from the one word you could not define, *crepuscule,* which means twilight or darkness.

It may not only be the new and unusual words that you will

have to look up. Some commonly used words can often be misdefined and so cause confusion.

This datum about not going past an undefined word is the most important fact in the whole subject of study. Every subject you have taken up and abandoned had its words which you failed to get defined.

Therefore, in studying this book be very, very certain you never go past a word you do not fully understand. If the material becomes confusing or you can't seem to grasp it, there will be a word just earlier that you have not understood. Don't go any further, but go back to BEFORE you got into trouble, find the misunderstood word and get it defined.

Definitions

As an aid to the reader, words most likely to be misunderstood have been defined in footnotes the first time they occur in the text. Words sometimes have several meanings. The footnote definitions in this book only give the meaning that the word has as it is used in the text. Other definitions for the word can be found in a dictionary.

A glossary including all the footnote definitions is at the back of this book.

Introduction

Scientology 0-8 means "Scientology, zero to infinity," the eight being the infinity sign turned upright.

This book is distilled information.

In more than fifty years of intense research into the behavior of man and ways to help man pull himself out of a degraded state, L. Ron Hubbard discovered the fundamental truths about the mind and spirit of man.

Certain truths that he discovered were central, senior data— the axioms,[1] codes and scales. These are the fundamentals and principles Ron used to develop all of our auditing procedures and applications of Scientology technology in life. *Scientology 0-8* is a reference book for Scientologists which contains these vital basics.

In preparing this new edition of *Scientology 0-8*, thorough research was carried out to ensure that all of the scales, codes and basic principles would be available in this book. As a result,

---

1. **axioms:** statements of natural laws on the order of those of the physical sciences.

Scientology 0-8 is now a more complete and better tool for students and Scientologists. Eighteen additional articles and scales have been added to this edition from L. Ron Hubbard's original writings and technical lectures.

It is with great pride that we present to you this new, updated edition of *Scientology 0-8: The Book of Basics.*

—**The Editors, 1988**

Table of Contents

1

A Description of Scientology

1

A Description of Scientology

Purpose

My purpose is to bring a barbarism out of the mud it thinks conceived it and to form, here on Earth, a civilization based on human understanding, not violence.

That's a big purpose. A broad field. A star-high goal.

But I think it's your purpose, too.

Religious and Philosophical Roots

We are on a much higher level in Scientology than the Western religions have been. And in our technologies, in the exactness of our understanding, we are on a much higher level than the great religious leaders of India who kept the spirit, the spiritual side of life, alive for thousands of years against all materialistic[1] ingression.[2]

What we are *doing* with this data *is* new. The way this material is organized *is* new. The technologies with which we

---

1. **materialistic:** of or concerning materialism, the opinion that only physical matter exists.

2. **ingression:** the action of entering; entrance.

can bring about a new state of being in man *are* new. But the basic idea, the basic hope of man as it appears today in Scientology, is thousands of years old.

And when we call Scientology a religion, we are calling it a religion out of a much deeper well than only the last two thousand years. It is a wisdom in the tradition of ten thousand years of search in Asia and in Western civilization.

Scientology treats the livingness[3] and beingness[4] of man and demonstrates to him a pathway to greater freedom. Scientology is an organization of the pertinences which are mutually held true by all men in all times and the development of technologies which demonstrate the existence of new phenomena[5] not hitherto[6] known, which are useful in creating states of beingness considered more desirable by man.

Subjects which I consulted in over a third of a century of organization and development of Scientology include the Veda;[7] the Tao of Lao-tse;[8] the Dharma[9] and the discourses of Gautama

---

3. **livingness:** the activity of going along a certain course, impelled (driven) by a purpose and with some place to arrive.

4. **beingness:** the assumption or choosing of a category of identity. Beingness is assumed by oneself or given to oneself or is attained. Examples of beingness would be one's own name, one's profession, one's physical characteristics, one's role in a game—each and all of these could be called one's beingness.

5. **phenomena:** observable facts or events.

6. **hitherto:** up to this time; until now.

7. **Veda:** the most ancient sacred writings of the Hindus.

8. **Tao of Lao-tse:** the Tao Teh King, or Tao Te Ching. The word *Tao* means "the way to solving the mystery which underlies all mysteries." Lao-tse (604–531 B.C.), its author, was one of the great philosophers of China.

9. **Dharma:** a body of scientific-philosophical-religious truth, written about 600 B.C. The Dharma rose up in Asia and its doctrines were spread to hundreds of millions of people by Gautama Buddha. Dharma was the name of a legendary Hindu sage—a mythological figure. The word means *knowingness,* or *lookingness.*

Buddha;[10] the general knowingness about life extant in the lamaseries[11] of the western hills of China; the technologies and beliefs of various barbaric cultures; the various materials of Christianity; the mathematical and technical methodologies[12] of the early Greeks, Romans and Arabians; the physical sciences, including the various speculations of Western philosophers such as Kant,[13] Nietzsche,[14] Schopenhauer,[15] Herbert Spencer[16] and Dewey,[17] and the various technologies extant in the civilizations of both the Orient[18] and the Occident[19] in the first half of the twentieth century.

But the philosopher ordinarily spends most of his working years in his ivory tower[20] and is pretty well insulated from life. To

---

10. **Gautama Buddha:** (563–483 B.C.) originally Gautama Sakyamuni, founder of the Buddhist religion. The term *Buddha* derives from *Bodhi*, or "one who has attained intellectual and ethical perfection by human means."

11. **lamaseries:** monasteries of the lamas (Buddhist monks of Tibet and Mongolia).

12. **methodologies:** systems of methods and procedures.

13. **Kant:** Immanuel Kant (1724–1804), German philosopher; sought to determine laws and limits of man's knowledge.

14. **Nietzsche:** Friedrich Wilhelm Nietzsche (1844–1900), German philosopher and poet. He denounced all religion and promoted the "morals of masters," the doctrine of perfecting man through forcible self-assertion and glorification of the "superman." His theories are regarded as having influenced the German attitudes in World War I and the Nazi regime.

15. **Schopenhauer:** Arthur Schopenhauer (1788–1860), German philosopher. He maintained that the desires and drives of men, as well as the forces of nature, are manifestations of a single will, specifically the will to live, which is the essence of the world. Since operation of the will means constant striving without satisfaction, life consists of suffering. Only by controlling the will through the intellect, by suppressing the desire to reproduce, can suffering be diminished.

16. **Herbert Spencer:** (1820–1903) English philosopher. He is known for his application of the doctrines of evolution to philosophy and ethics.

17. **Dewey:** John Dewey (1859–1952), American philosopher and educator.

18. **Orient:** the East; countries east of the Mediterranean, especially East Asia.

19. **Occident:** the part of the world west of Asia, especially Europe and the Americas.

20. **ivory tower:** figuratively, a place of mental withdrawal from reality and action.

---

know life you've got to be part of life, you must get down there and *look*, you must get into the nooks and crannies of existence, and you must rub elbows with all kinds and types of men before you can finally establish what man is. I lived with bandits in Mongolia and hunted with Pygmies in the Philippines—as a matter of fact I studied twenty-one different primitive races, including the white race—and my conclusions were that man, regardless of his state or culture, was essentially the same, that he was a spiritual being pulled down into the material, and I concluded finally that he needed a hand.

The Dynamic[21] Principle of Existence

In 1932 I undertook an investigation to determine the dynamic principle of existence in a workable form which might lead to the resolution of some of the problems of mankind. My long research in ancient and modern philosophy culminated[22] in 1938. A work was written at that time which embraced man and his activities.

In the following years I researched further in order to prove or disprove the axioms so established.

My first effort was to find a common denominator[23] to all men. I had seen man in both his more primitive states and his highly cultured states, and I knew that if we could isolate a common denominator that embraced all men, then perhaps from that we could unlock this riddle.

---

21. **dynamic:** of or relating to the motivating or driving force, physical or moral, in any field.

22. **culminated:** ended or arrived at a final stage.

23. **common denominator:** a quality, opinion or other attribute shared by all the persons or things in a group.

After exhaustive research, I isolated one word which embraced the finite[24] universe as a dynamic principle of existence.

I discovered that the common denominator—the dynamic principle—was *survive*. Whatever else man was trying to do, whether he was cultured or primitive, he was attempting to survive. Well, what of such things as morals, ideals, love? Don't these things go above "mere survival"? Unfortunately or fortunately, they do not. Ideals, honesty, love of one's fellow man— one cannot find good survival for one or for many where these things are absent. Even the most esoteric[25] concepts fall within this understanding of survival.

Survival is not a matter of being alive this moment and dead the next. Survival is actually a graduated scale.[26]

This dynamic principle can be subdivided into eight main drive lines, or dynamics, which are held in common with man.

The first dynamic is the urge toward survival of self.

The second dynamic is the urge toward survival through sex or children.

The third dynamic is the urge toward survival through a group of individuals or as a group.

The fourth dynamic is the urge toward survival through all mankind and as mankind.

---

24. **finite:** having bounds or limits; not infinite; measurable.

25. **esoteric:** intended only for people with special knowledge or interest.

26. **graduated scale:** (also called a *gradient scale*) a scale of condition graduated from zero to infinity. On a scale of survival, everything above zero or center would be more and more survival, approaching an infinite survival (immortality), and everything below zero or center would be more and more nonsurvival, approaching an infinite nonsurvival (death). Absolutes are considered to be unobtainable.

The fifth dynamic is the urge toward survival through life forms such as animals, birds, insects, fish and vegetation, and is the urge to survive as these.

The sixth dynamic is the urge toward survival as the physical universe and has as its components *Matter*, *Energy*, *Space* and *Time* (from which we derive the word MEST).

The seventh dynamic is the urge toward survival through spirits or as a spirit. Anything spiritual, with or without identity, would come under the seventh dynamic. A subheading of this dynamic is ideas and concepts such as beauty, and the desire to survive through these.

The eighth dynamic is the urge toward survival through a Supreme Being, or more exactly, infinity.

Dianetics and Scientology

Covering the first *four* of these dynamics, Dianetics became, of all the past studies of man, *the* grandpa, the immediate ancestor of Scientology. Dianetics was the basic discovery which led to and was the reason for Scientology.

Dianetics comes from the Greek words *dia* (through) and *noos* (soul). Dianetics is *what the soul is doing to the body*. It is the route from aberrated (or aberrated and ill) human to a well, happy, high-IQ human being. This breakthrough had never before been achieved in man's history.

None of the postulates and early discoveries in this research outlawed any concept concerning the human soul or divine or creative imagination. The optimum survival conduct pattern was formulated and then studied for exceptions, and there were no exceptions found. It was understood perfectly that Dianetics was a study in the finite universe only and that spheres and realms of thought and action might well exist above this finite sphere. But it was also discovered that none of these factors were needed to resolve the entire problem of human aberration[27] and irrational conduct.

The human mind was found to have been most grossly maligned,[28] because man had not been able to distinguish between irrational conduct derived from poor data and irrational conduct derived from another, far more vicious source.

I discovered the *reactive mind*. It had managed to bury itself from view so thoroughly that only inductive[29] philosophy, traveling from effect back to cause, served to uncover it.

The reactive mind is a portion of a person's mind which works on a totally stimulus-response[30] basis, which is not under his volitional[31] control and which exerts force and the power of command over his awareness, purposes, thoughts, body and actions.

Stored in the reactive mind are *engrams*, and here I found the single source of human aberrations and psychosomatic[32] ills.

---

27. **aberration:** a departure from rational thought or behavior. From the Latin, *aberrare,* to wander from; Latin, *ab,* away, *errare,* to wander. It means basically to err, to make mistakes, or more specifically to have fixed ideas which are not true. Aberration is opposed to sanity, which would be its opposite.

28. **maligned:** spoken evilly of; slandered.

29. **inductive:** of or relating to induction, a way of reasoning using known facts to produce general laws.

30. **stimulus-response:** given a certain stimulus something will automatically give a certain response.

31. **volitional:** of or having to do with the use of one's own will in choosing or making a decision, etc.

32. **psychosomatic:** *psycho* refers to mind and *somatic* refers to body; the term *psychosomatic* means the mind making the body ill or illnesses which have been created physically within the body by derangement of the mind.

An engram is *a complete recording, down to the last accurate detail, of every perception present in a moment of partial or full unconsciousness.*

In all laboratory tests, engrams were found to possess "inexhaustible" sources of power to command the body.

The dynamics are inhibited by engrams, which lie across them and disperse life force. Intelligence is inhibited by engrams which feed false or improperly graded data to the mind.

Thus, the isolation and resolution of the reactive mind was a major breakthrough for man. The exact moment of the breakthrough is recorded at the public level with the book *Dianetics: The Modern Science of Mental Health.*

Man had no inkling[33] whatever of Dianetics. None. This was the bolt from the blue.[34] Man was hacking and sawing and shocking and injecting and teaching and moralizing and counseling and hanging and jailing men with enthusiasm without any idea at all of what caused man to behave as he did or what made him sick or well.

The answer was and still is Dianetics. It is man's most advanced school of the *mind.*

Scientology is the route to total freedom and ability as a spiritual being. It is the study and handling of the spirit in relationship to itself, universes and other life.

---

33. **inkling:** hint; a slight knowledge or suspicion.
34. **bolt from the blue:** a sudden, unforeseen occurrence.

Oddly enough, the step from a human being to a spirit had been achieved, if rarely—Buddhism, other spiritual practices, even Christianity—but it was not generally credited. Scientology *really* achieves it and for the first time with *total* stability, no relapse[35] and, invariably, one for one.

Nevertheless, man had an inkling of the *goals* of Scientology even though he considered them almost beyond God.

Handling Life with Scientology

There are two distinct divisions in Scientology. The first is philosophic, the second is technical. Under the philosophic heading one discovers the ways and means of forming new ways of life and evaluating or creating standards of livingness and beingness. Scientology concludes and demonstrates certain truths. These truths might be considered to be the highest common denominators of existence itself. They have the aspect of precision observations rather than philosophic hazardings.[36] When treated as precision observations, many results occur. When regarded as philosophic opinions, only more philosophy results.

By this knowingness alone and without processing[37] (individual technical applications), it should be understood clearly that a new way of life could be created or an old way of life could be understood and better endured or altered.

---

35. **relapse:** the act or instance of slipping or falling back into a former condition, especially after improvement.

36. **hazardings:** offerings of statements, conjectures, etc.

37. **processing:** the application of Dianetics or Scientology processes to someone by a trained auditor. The exact definition of processing is: The action of asking a preclear a question (which he can understand and answer), getting an answer to that question and acknowledging him for that answer. Also called auditing.

Under the technical division we have a long series of developed processes[38] which, applied immediately and directly to life or an organism thereof, produce desirable changes in the conditions of life. This division comprises Applied Scientology or Scientology Applied Philosophy and contains *standard technology.*[39]

I looked early and long at man to find out what methods he used to survive, how he adapted himself to environments in his attempt at survival, and what I found was that man advanced to the degree that he preserved his spiritual integrity,[40] that he preserved his values, that he remained honest, that he remained decent—and I found that he disintegrated or deteriorated to the degree that he abandoned these things.

The average man is up against problems. He is asking himself, "How can I make more money? How can I make my wife faithful to me? How can I help my children grow up?" These questions absorb a tremendous quantity of his energy. But he can't do anything about it because he is so immersed in it. So in Scientology processing he resolves these questions, he understands what he's doing, and he turns from a man who is simply a puzzled static[41] being into somebody who is more than that.

We see governments and societies desperately trying to help

---

38. **processes:** sets of questions asked or commands given by an auditor to help a person find out things about himself or life and to improve his condition.

39. **standard technology:** the exact processes and auditing actions laid down by L. Ron Hubbard and used for the invariable resolution of cases, taught in the organizations of Scientology and used without variation by all Scientology auditors. The term applies equally to Dianetics and its technology.

40. **integrity:** adherence to moral and ethical principles; soundness of moral character; honesty. It comes from the Latin word *integritas,* meaning untouched, undivided, whole.

41. **static:** not changing.

man. They are trying, however, to solve his problems *for* him, and their efforts to do this have not resulted in any great advance for man.

The real work is to put an individual into a mental condition where he can confront his own problems and solve them—to put him in a position where he can confront life better, where his reaction time is better, where he can identify the factors in his life more easily. And so he looks around, starts solving his own problems and betters his own life. That is an essential difference between Scientology and other efforts to help man.

We have in the technical division of Scientology basically two activities—processing and training.

Scientology processing (auditing) is done on the principle of making an individual look at his own existence and improve his ability to confront what he is and where he is. An *auditor*[42] is the person trained in the technology and whose job it is to ask the person to look and get him to do so.

There is a large technology for this, but essentially an auditor has to be able to get his questions answered and the individual who is being processed finally has to answer the questions. The question is asked until it is totally answered and the person is totally aware that he has answered it.

As people come into Scientology (and they are coming in, in very swiftly increasing numbers, all over the world), normally what they do first is read a book, and then they may read quite a few books, and go around and about Scientology for some time.

---

42. **auditor:** a person trained and qualified in applying Dianetics and/or Scientology processes and procedures to individuals for their betterment; called an auditor because *auditor* means "one who listens."

They attend some of the introductory courses, and then they get some processing—often beginning with Dianetics. Their IQ goes up, their abilities increase, they become more capable of handling their lives.

And when one then decides to be an auditor, he or she goes to an Academy[43] of Scientology and studies and learns how to audit and so help others.

You will find throughout Scientology that the gradient approach is a primary and regulating factor. And a gradient approach has been very, very important in this line of research. The principle is incidentally quite new. The *essence* of a gradient is just being able to do a little bit more and a little bit more and a little bit more until you finally make the grade.[44]

Creating a New World

We live in a world that is desperately in need of some good order. It isn't aberration on our part that we say some things ought to be changed. Actually I rarely tell you that things should be changed; I simply tell you that a world has to be created. I don't even assume that one exists. I figure that this one is on its way out and that somebody had better put one in its place. Just how we go about doing that is up to you and up to me.

People think of professional practitioners[45] as doctors, who, aloof[46] from other concerns, practice on the sick. This is a very

---

43. **Academy:** the part of a Scientology church in which auditing courses and training are delivered.

44. **make the grade:** overcome obstacles and succeed.

45. **practitioners:** people who practice a profession, art, etc.

46. **aloof:** at a distance, especially in feeling or interest; apart.

novel[47] idea, however. It was dreamed up, probably, by the first lazy witch doctor and used forever thereafter by most mental specialists. I want to banish that idea from amongst us all.

If we are doctors (by which might be meant "repairers"), then we are doctors on the third and fourth dynamics, the dynamics of groups and mankind as a whole, and we handle the first (self) and the second (sex and family) only to achieve better function on the third and fourth.

The third and fourth dynamics subdivide. Any third dynamic breaks down into many activities and professions—a neighborhood, a business concern, a military group, a city government, etc. The fourth breaks down, just now, mainly to races and nations.

We find ourselves, for instance, today, with the job of cleaning up the whole field of mental health. That is at least what it calls itself. Mental "health" has been perverted for something over half a century into an excuse for a Belsen[48] or an Auschwitz.[49] It's an operating climate of danger and chaos. That field couldn't even begin to clean itself up. It was unaware of or cold to human rights. It had no technology that worked, upon which to base any actual professional ethics. As we do in Scientology have the technology and the ethics, we inherited the job.

Where we have made the breakthrough in Scientology and where we have made progress, we have done so in accomplishing the goals which man has had as long as he has been man.

---

47. **novel:** of a new kind.

48. **Belsen:** village in West Germany; the site of a Nazi concentration camp and extermination center.

49. **Auschwitz:** city in southwest Poland; site of a Nazi concentration camp notorious as an extermination center.

What he has considered good and what he has considered desirable in the field of philosophy, we have accomplished technically. We have now arrived in Scientology at a point where man should have been for the last five thousand years. There has never been this technology before. You are in a very fortunate position of not having to develop the technology of auditing. A good auditor has found this out. He uses the tools he's got and he uses them well. There is a tremendous amount of understanding involved here. There are millions of words written on the subject of auditing technology. An auditor can be pretty staggered to suddenly realize how much he really knows.

Auditors are dedicated and sincere in getting this job done. There has never been a more sincere group on the face of the Earth than those who are in the ranks of Scientology auditors. We wouldn't have started on auditing if we weren't good people who wanted to help our fellow man. We are the first people to appear on Earth since its first solidification out of nebulous[50] vaporings[51] who can get this job done, and who *really* know what we are doing.

The very truth that we know, its simplicity and ease of grasp, the very honesty with which we approach our task, give us probably the largest barriers we have to overcome. Man has been defrauded so often, persuaded so wrongly, and has returned to the same old rut so inevitably and in such a defeated frame of mind, that he is not able to grasp easily the firm and friendly hand of the auditor which is being reached out to him.

---

50. **nebulous:** unclear, vague or indefinite.

51. **vaporings:** instances or occurrences of vapor, a gaseous form of any substance which is usually a liquid or a solid.

The Aims of Scientology

A civilization without insanity, without criminals and without war, where the able can prosper and honest beings can have rights, and where man is free to rise to greater heights, are the aims of Scientology.

Nonpolitical in nature, Scientology welcomes any individual of any creed,[52] race or nation.

We seek no revolution. We seek only evolution to higher states of being for the individual and for society.

We are achieving our aims.

After endless millennia of ignorance about himself, his mind and the universe, a breakthrough has been made for man.

Other efforts man has made have been surpassed.

The combined truths of fifty thousand years of thinking men, distilled and amplified by new discoveries about man, have made for this success.

We welcome you to Scientology. We only expect of you your help in achieving our aims and helping others. We expect you to be helped.

Scientology is the most vital movement on Earth today.

In a turbulent world, the job is not easy. But then, if it were, we wouldn't have to be doing it.

---

52. **creed:** a statement of belief, principles or opinions on any subject; a brief statement of religious belief.

We respect man and believe he is worthy of help. We respect you and believe you, too, can help.

Scientology does not owe its help. We have done nothing to cause us to propitiate.[53] Had we done so, we would not now be bright enough to do what we are doing.

Man suspects all offers of help. He has often been betrayed, his confidence shattered. Too frequently he has given his trust and been betrayed. We may err, for we build a world with broken straws. But we will never betray your faith in us so long as you are one of us.

The sun never sets on Scientology.

And may a new day dawn for you, for those you love and for man.

Our aims are simple, if great.

And we will succeed, and are succeeding at each new revolution of the Earth.

Your help is acceptable to us.

Our help is yours.

---

53. **propitiate:** attempt to appease or buy off some danger or imagined danger.

2

The Scientology Symbol

2

The Scientology Symbol

The "S and Double Triangle" symbol is the symbol of Scientology.

There are two triangles, over which the S is imposed.

The S simply stands for Scientology, which is derived from *scio* (knowing in the fullest sense).

The two triangles are as follows:

The ARC Triangle

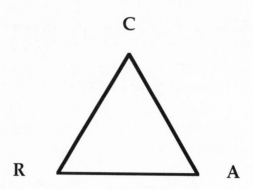

The lower triangle in the Scientology symbol is called the A-R-C triangle.

ARC is a word made from the initial letters of Affinity, Reality and Communication, which together equate to understanding. It is pronounced by stating its letters: A-R-C.

To Scientologists, it has come to mean good feeling, love or friendliness, such as "He was in ARC with his friend."

One does not, however, fall out of ARC; he has an ARC break: a sudden drop or cutting of one's affinity, reality or communication with someone or something. Upsets with people or things come about because of the lessening or sundering[1] of affinity, reality or communication or understanding. It's called an *ARC break* instead of an upset because if one discovers which of the three points of understanding have been cut, one can bring about a rapid recovery in the person's state of mind.

---

1. **sundering:** breaking or tearing apart; severing.

Of the three, *communication* is by far the most important. Affinity and reality exist to further communication.

The triangle of affinity, reality and communication could be called an interactive triangle in that no point of it can be raised without affecting the other two points and raising them, and no point of it can be lowered without affecting the other two points.

When we speak of affinity, reality and communication we are talking about the three component parts of life. These three quantities in combination playing upon MEST give us the manifestation we might call computation, or understanding. One has to have some affinity for an object, some communication with it and some concept of its reality before he can understand it. His ability to understand any thought or object depends upon his affinity, his communication and his reality.

For instance, there must be good affinity (which is to say affection) between two people before they are very real to each other. There must be good affinity between two people before they can talk together with any truth or confidence. Before two people can be real to each other there must be some communication between them. They must at least see each other, which is itself a form of communication. Before two people can feel any affinity for each other they must, to some degree, be real.

It is only necessary to improve one corner of this very valuable triangle in Scientology in order to improve the remaining two corners. It is only necessary to improve two corners of the triangle to improve the third.

This is about the most important data I have ever run across in the field of interpersonal relations, control and management.

The KRC Triangle

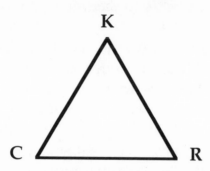

The upper triangle is the KRC triangle. The points are K for Knowledge, R for Responsibility and C for Control.

It is difficult to be responsible for something or control something unless you have *knowledge* of it.

It is folly to try to control something or even know something without *responsibility*.

It is hard to fully know something or be responsible for something over which you have no *control*, otherwise the result can be an overwhelm.

A being can of course run away from life (blow) and go sit on the backside of the moon and do nothing and think nothing. In which case he would need to know nothing, be responsible for nothing and control nothing. He would also be unhappy and he definitely would be dead so far as himself and all else was concerned. But, as you can't kill a thetan,[2] the state is impossible to maintain and the road back can be gruesome.

---

2. **thetan:** what we call the living unit in Scientology. Taken from the Greek letter *theta*, the mathematical symbol used in Scientology to indicate the source of life and life itself. It is the individual, the being; that which is aware of being aware; the identity which is the individual. The thetan is most familiar to one and all as "you."

The route up from death or apathy or inaction is to *know* something about it, take some *responsibility* for the state one is in and the scene, and *control* oneself to a point where some control is put into the scene to make it go right. Then *know* why it went wrong, take *responsibility* for it, and *control* it enough to make it go more toward an ideal scene.[3]

Little by little one can make anything go right by:

Increasing knowledge on all dynamics;

Increasing responsibility on all dynamics;

Increasing control on all dynamics.

If one sorts out any situation one finds oneself in on this basis, he will generally succeed.

Field Marshal Montgomery[4] was supposed to have said that leadership was composed of "knowledge, willpower, initiative[5] and courage." These are assumed qualities in a man. This was good advice but offered no road out or no avenue of *increase* in capability.

The KRC triangle acts like the ARC triangle. When one corner is increased the other two also rise.

---

3. **ideal scene:** how something ought to be. The entire concept of an ideal scene is a clean statement of its purpose.

4. **Field Marshal Montgomery:** Sir Bernard Law Montgomery (1887–1976), British field marshal in World War II. He commanded the British army which drove the Germans out of Egypt and was later the commander of the Allied armies in Northern France. Made chief of the British general staff in 1946. [*Field marshal:* an officer next in rank to the commander in chief in the British, French, German and some other armies.]

5. **initiative:** the characteristic of originating new ideas or methods; ability to think and act without being urged; enterprise.

Most thetans have a dreadfully bad opinion of their capabilities compared to what they actually are. Hardly any thetan believes himself capable of what he is really capable of accomplishing.

By inching up each corner of the KRC triangle bit by bit, ignoring the losses and making the wins firm, a being at length discovers his power and command of life.

The second triangle of the symbol of Scientology is well worth knowing. It is particularly applicative[6] to an executive but applies to all Scientologists.

It interacts best when used with high ARC. Thus the triangles interlock.

It is for *use* as well as all of Scientology.

---

6. **applicative:** applying or capable of being applied, as to some practical use.

3

Consideration and Mechanics

3

Consideration[1] and Mechanics[2]

[1954]

Considerations take rank over the mechanics of space, energy and time. By this it is meant that an idea or opinion is, fundamentally, superior to space, energy and time, or organizations of form, since it is conceived that space, energy and time are themselves broadly agreed-upon considerations. That so many minds agree brings about reality in the form of space, energy and time. These mechanics, then, of space, energy and time are the product of agreed-upon considerations mutually held by life.

This aspect of existence when viewed from the level of man, however, is a reverse of the greater truth above, for man works on the secondary opinion that mechanics are real, and that his own personal considerations are less important than space, energy and time. This is an inversion.[3] These mechanics of space, energy and time, the forms, objects and combinations

---

1. **consideration:** thinking, believing, supposing, postulating. Consideration is the highest capability of life, taking rank over the mechanics of space, energy and time.

2. **mechanics:** referring to space, energy, objects and time. When something has those things in it, it constitutes something mechanical.

3. **inversion:** a switch to an opposite obsessive consideration, such as from compulsion to inhibition.

---

thereof, have taken such precedence[4] in man that they have become more important than considerations as such, and so his ability is overpowered and he is unable to act freely in the framework of mechanics. Man, therefore, has an inverted view. Whereas considerations such as those he daily makes are the actual source of space, energy, time and forms, man is operating so as not to alter his basic considerations; he therefore invalidates himself by supposing another determinism of space, energy, time and form. Although he is part of that which created these, he gives them such strength and validity that his own considerations thereafter must fall subordinate to space, energy, time and form, and so he cannot alter the universe in which he dwells.

The freedom of an individual depends upon that individual's freedom to alter his considerations of space, energy, time and forms of life and his roles in it. If he cannot change his mind about these, he is then fixed and enslaved amidst barriers such as those of the physical universe, and barriers of his own creation. Man thus is seen to be enslaved by barriers of his own creation. He creates these barriers himself, or by agreeing with things which hold these barriers to be actual.

There is a basic series of assumptions in processing, which assumptions do not alter the philosophy of Scientology. The first of these assumptions is that man can have a greater freedom. The second is that so long as he remains relatively sane, he desires a greater freedom. And the third assumption is that the auditor desires to deliver a greater freedom to that person with whom he is working. If these assumptions are not agreed upon and are not used, then auditing degenerates into "the observation of effect," which is, of course, a goalless, soulless pursuit, and is, indeed, a pursuit which has degraded what is called modern science.

---

4. **precedence:** priority in time or order.

The goal of processing is to bring an individual into such thorough communication with the physical universe that he can regain the power and ability of his own considerations (postulates).

A Scientologist is one who understands life. His technical skill is devoted to the resolution of the problems of life.

4

The Original Axioms of Dianetics

The Primary Axioms of Dianetics

[1948]

Axiom 1:   *Survive!*

Axiom 2:   *The purpose of the mind is to solve problems relating to survival.*

Axiom 3:   *The mind directs the organism, the species,[1] its symbiotes[2] or life in the effort of survival.*

Axiom 4:   *The mind, as the central direction system of the body, poses, perceives and resolves problems of survival and directs or fails to direct their execution.*

Axiom 5:   *The persistency of the individual in life is directly governed by the strength of his basic dynamic.*

Axiom 6:   *Intelligence is the ability of an individual, group or race to resolve problems relating to survival.*

---

1. **species:** a group of animals or plants that have certain permanent characteristics in common.

2. **symbiotes:** any or all life or energy forms which are mutually dependent for survival. The atom depends on the universe, the universe on the atom.

The Fundamental Axioms of Dianetics

[1950]

*The dynamic principle of existence is **Survive!***

Survival, considered as the single and sole purpose, subdivides into four *dynamics.*

Dynamic one is the urge of the individual toward survival for the individual and his symbiotes. (By *symbiote* is meant all entities[1] and energies which aid survival.)

Dynamic two is the urge of the individual toward survival through procreation;[2] it includes both the sex act and the raising of progeny,[3] the care of children and their symbiotes.

Dynamic three is the urge of the individual toward survival for the group or the group for the group and includes the symbiotes of that group.

Dynamic four is the urge of the individual toward survival

---

1. **entities:** beings; existences.

2. **procreation:** bringing (a living thing) into existence by the natural process of reproduction; generation.

3. **progeny:** offspring; descendants.

for mankind or the urge toward survival of mankind for mankind as well as the group for mankind, etc., and includes the symbiotes of mankind.

The *absolute goal* of survival is immortality or infinite survival. This is sought by the individual in terms of himself as an organism, as a spirit or as a name or as his children, as a group of which he is a member or as mankind and the progeny and symbiotes of others as well as his own.

The reward of survival activity is *pleasure*.

The ultimate penalty of destructive activity is death or complete nonsurvival, and is *pain*.

Successes raise the survival potential toward infinite survival.

Failures lower the survival potential toward death.

The human mind is engaged upon perceiving and retaining data, composing or computing conclusions and posing and resolving problems related to organisms along all four dynamics; and the purpose of perception, retention, concluding and resolving problems is to direct its own organism and symbiotes and other organisms and symbiotes along the four dynamics toward survival.

Intelligence is the ability to perceive, pose and resolve problems.

The *dynamic* is the tenacity to life and vigor and persistence in survival.

Both the dynamic and intelligence are necessary to persist and accomplish and neither is a constant quantity from individual to individual, group to group.

The *dynamics* are inhibited by engrams, which lie across them and disperse life force.

Intelligence is inhibited by engrams which feed false or improperly graded data into the analyzer.[4]

Happiness is the overcoming of not unknown obstacles toward a known goal and, transiently,[5] the contemplation of or indulgence in pleasure.

The *analytical mind* is that portion of the mind which perceives and retains experience data to compose and resolve problems and direct the organism along the four dynamics. *It thinks in differences and similarities.*

The *reactive mind* is that portion of the mind which files and retains physical pain and painful emotion and seeks to direct the organism solely on a stimulus-response basis. *It thinks only in identities.*

The *somatic mind* is that mind which, directed by the analytical or reactive mind, places solutions into effect on the physical level.

A *training pattern* is that stimulus-response mechanism resolved by the analytical mind to care for routine activity or

---

4. **analyzer:** the analytical mind: that portion of the mind which perceives and retains experience data to compose and resolve problems.

5. **transiently:** fleetingly; temporarily; briefly.

emergency activity. It is held in the somatic mind and can be changed at will by the analytical mind.

Habit is that stimulus-response reaction dictated by the reactive mind from the content of engrams and put into effect by the somatic mind. It can be changed only by those things which change engrams.

Aberrations, under which is included all deranged or irrational behavior, are caused by engrams. They are stimulus-response, pro- and contra-survival.

Psychosomatic ills are caused by engrams.

The *engram* is the single source of aberrations and psychosomatic ills.

Moments of "unconsciousness" when the analytical mind is attenuated[6] in greater or lesser degree are the only moments when engrams can be received.

The *engram* is a moment of "unconsciousness" containing physical pain or painful emotion and all perceptions, and is not available to the analytical mind as experience.

Emotion is three things: engramic response to situations, endocrine[7] metering of the body to meet situations on an analytical level and the inhibition or the furtherance[8] of life force.

---

6. **attenuated:** weakened; reduced in force or in value.

7. **endocrine:** of or relating to the endocrine system, a group of glands which secrete hormones directly into the bloodstream which influence or regulate other organs in the body.

8. **furtherance:** the act of furthering; advancement.

The *potential value* of an individual or a group may be expressed by the equation

$$PV = ID^x$$

where I is Intelligence and D is Dynamic.

The *worth* of an individual is computed in terms of the alignment, on any dynamic, of his potential value with optimum survival along that dynamic. A high PV may, by reversed vector,[9] result in a negative worth as in some severely aberrated persons. A high PV on any dynamic *assures* a high worth only in the unaberrated person.

---

9. **vector:** a physical quantity with both magnitude and direction, such as a force or velocity.

5

The Logics
and
Dianetic Axioms

The Logics[1]

[1951]

Logic 1:   *Knowledge is a whole group or subdivision of a group of data or speculations or conclusions on data or methods of gaining data.*

Logic 2:   *A body of knowledge is a body of data, aligned or unaligned, or methods of gaining data.*

Logic 3:   *Any knowledge which can be sensed, measured or experienced by any entity is capable of influencing that entity.*
COROLLARY:[2] That knowledge which cannot be sensed, measured or experienced by any entity or type of entity cannot influence that entity or type of entity.

Logic 4:   *A datum is a symbol of matter, energy, space or time, or any combination thereof, in any universe, or the*

---

1. **Logics:** a method of thinking. They apply to any universe or any thinking process. They are the forms of thought behavior which can, but do not necessarily have to, be used in creating universes.

2. **corollary:** a natural consequence or result; something that follows logically after something else is proved.

matter, energy, space or time itself, or any combination thereof, in any universe.[3]

Logic 5: *A definition of terms is necessary to the alignment, statement and resolution of suppositions, observations, problems and solutions and their communication.*

DEFINITION: Descriptive definition: one which classifies by characteristics,[4] by describing existing states of being.

DEFINITION: Differentiative[5] definition: one which compares unlikeness to existing states of being or not-being.

DEFINITION: Associative[6] definition: one which declares likeness to existing states of being or not-being.

DEFINITION: Action definition: one which delineates[7] cause and potential change of state of being by cause of existence, inexistence, action, inaction, purpose or lack of purpose.

Logic 6: *Absolutes are unobtainable.*

Logic 7: *Gradient scales are necessary to the evaluation of problems and their data.*

This is the tool of infinity-valued logic: Absolutes

---

3. Originally stated as *"A datum is a facsimile of states of being, states of not-being, actions or inactions, conclusions or suppositions in the physical or any other universe,"* this Logic was corrected in the lecture of 10 November 1952, "Logics 1–7."

4. **characteristics:** distinguishing traits, features or qualities.

5. **differentiative:** having to do with the ability to "tell the difference" between one person and another, one object and another.

6. **associative:** tending to connect, bring into relation or unite.

7. **delineates:** describes in words; portrays.

are unobtainable. Terms such as good and bad, alive and dead, right and wrong, are used only in conjunction[8] with gradient scales. On the scale of right and wrong, everything above zero or center would be more and more right, approaching an infinite rightness, and everything below center would be more and more wrong, approaching infinite wrongness. All things assisting the survival of the survivor are right for the survivor. All things inhibiting survival from the viewpoint of the survivor can be considered wrong for the survivor. The more a thing assists survival, the more it can be considered right for the survivor; the more a thing or action inhibits survival, the more it is wrong from the viewpoint of the intended survivor.

COROLLARY: Any datum has only relative truth.

COROLLARY: Truth is relative to environments, experience and truth.

Logic 8: *A datum can be evaluated only by a datum of comparable magnitude.[9]*

Logic 9: *A datum is as valuable as it has been evaluated.*

Logic 10: *The value of a datum is established by the amount of alignment (relationship) it imparts to other data.*

Logic 11: *The value of a datum or field of data can be established by its degree of assistance in survival or its inhibition to survival.*

---

8. **conjunction:** combination; union.

9. **magnitude:** greatness of size, extent, importance or influence.

Logic 12:   *The value of a datum or a field of data is modified by the viewpoint of the observer.*

Logic 13:   *Problems are resolved by compartmenting them into areas of similar magnitude and data, comparing them to data already known or partially known, and resolving each area. Data which cannot be known immediately may be resolved by addressing what is known and using its solution to resolve the remainder.*

Logic 14:   *Factors introduced into a problem or solution which do not derive from natural law but only from authoritarian command aberrate that problem or solution.*

Logic 15:   *The introduction of an arbitrary[10] into a problem or solution invites the further introduction of arbitraries into problems and solutions.*

Logic 16:   *An abstract[11] postulate must be compared to the universe to which it applies and brought into the category of things which can be sensed, measured or experienced in that universe before such postulate can be considered workable.*

Logic 17:   *Those fields which most depend upon authoritative[12] opinion for their data least contain known natural law.*

Logic 18:   *A postulate is as valuable as it is workable.*

---

10. **arbitrary:** something which is introduced into a situation without regard to the data of the situation.

11. **abstract:** theoretical rather than practical.

12. **authoritative:** having the support or weight of authority; accepted by most authorities in a field.

Logic 19: *The workability of a postulate is established by the degree to which it explains existing phenomena already known, by the degree that it predicts new phenomena which when looked for will be found to exist, and by the degree that it does not require that phenomena which do not exist in fact be called into existence for its explanation.*

Logic 20: *A science may be considered to be a large body of aligned data which has similarity in application and which has been deduced[13] or induced[14] from basic postulates.*

Logic 21: *Mathematics are methods of postulating or resolving real or abstract data in any universe and integrating[15] by symbolization of data, postulates and resolutions.*

Logic 22: *The human mind* is an observer, postulator, creator and storage place of knowledge.*
*The human mind by definition includes the awareness unit of the living organism, the observer, the computer of data, the spirit, the memory storage, the life force and the individual motivator[16] of the living organism. It is used as distinct from the brain which can be considered to be motivated by the mind.

---

13. **deduced:** inferred from a general rule or principle; reached (a conclusion) by reasoning.

14. **induced:** reasoned in such a way as to produce general laws through known facts.

15. **integrating:** putting or bringing (parts) together into a whole; unifying.

16. **motivator:** that thing which moves, rouses, urges on.

Logic 23:   *The human mind is a servomechanism*[17] *to any mathematics evolved*[18] *or employed by the human mind.*

POSTULATE: The human mind and inventions of the human mind are capable of resolving any and all problems which can be sensed, measured or experienced directly or indirectly.

COROLLARY: The human mind is capable of resolving the problem of the human mind.

The borderline of solution of this science lies between *why* life is surviving and *how* life is surviving. It is possible to resolve *how* life is surviving without resolving *why* life is surviving.

Logic 24:   *The resolution of the philosophical, scientific and human studies (such as economics, politics, sociology, medicine, criminology, etc.) depends primarily upon the resolution of the problems of the human mind.*

NOTE: The primary step in resolving the broad activities of man could be considered to be the resolving of the activities of the mind itself. Hence, the Logics carry to this point and then proceed as axioms concerning the human mind, such axioms being substantiated[19] as relative truths by much newly discovered phenomena. The ensuing[20] axioms, from Logic 24, apply no less to the various "ologies"[21] than they do to deaberrating[22]

---

17. **servomechanism:** a device which is set in motion by another mechanism and monitors the operation or power of the operating mechanism by the way in which it operates.

18. **evolved:** developed or worked out gradually.

19. **substantiated:** supported with evidence; proven.

20. **ensuing:** following immediately.

21. **"ologies":** branches of learning; sciences (a humorous usage).

22. **deaberrating:** removing aberration. *See also* **aberration** in the glossary.

or improving the operation of the mind. It should not be thought that the following axioms are devoted to the construction of anything as limited as a therapy, which is only incidental to the resolution of human aberration and such things as psychosomatic illnesses. These axioms are capable of such solution, as has been demonstrated, but such a narrow application would indicate a very narrow scope of view.

The Axioms of Dianetics

[1951]

Axiom 1: The source of life is a static[1] of peculiar and particular properties.

Axiom 2: At least a portion of the static called life is impinged[2] upon the physical universe.

Axiom 3: That portion of the static of life which is impinged upon the physical universe has for its dynamic goal, survival and only survival.

Axiom 4: The physical universe is reducible to motion of energy operating in space through time.

Axiom 5: That portion of the static of life concerned with the life organisms of the physical universe is concerned wholly with motion.

Axiom 6: The life static has as one of its properties the ability to mobilize and animate matter into living organisms.

---

1. **static:** something that has no mass, no location and no position in time, and which has no wavelength at all.

2. **impinged:** struck, hit or dashed (on, upon or against something).

Axiom 7: The life static is engaged in a conquest of the physical universe.

Axiom 8: The life static conquers the material universe by learning and applying the physical laws of the physical universe.

SYMBOL: The symbol for the LIFE STATIC in use hereafter is the Greek letter THETA.

Axiom 9: A fundamental operation of THETA in surviving is bringing order into the chaos of the physical universe.

Axiom 10: THETA brings order into chaos by conquering whatever in MEST may be prosurvival and destroying whatever in MEST may be contrasurvival, at least through the medium of life organisms.

SYMBOL: The symbol for the PHYSICAL UNIVERSE in use hereafter is MEST, from the first letters of the words MATTER, ENERGY, SPACE and TIME, or the Greek letter PHI.

Axiom 11: A life organism is composed of matter and energy in space and time, animated by THETA.

SYMBOL: Living organism or organisms will hereafter be represented by the Greek letter LAMBDA.

Axiom 12: The MEST part of the organism follows the laws of the physical sciences. All LAMBDA is concerned with motion.

Axiom 13: THETA operating through LAMBDA converts the forces of the physical universe into forces to conquer the physical universe.

Axiom 14: THETA *working upon physical universe motion must maintain a harmonious[3] rate of motion.*

The limits of LAMBDA are narrow, both as to thermal[4] and mechanical motion.

Axiom 15: LAMBDA *is the intermediate[5] step in the conquest of the physical universe.*

Axiom 16: *The basic food of any organism consists of light and chemicals.*

Organisms can exist only as higher levels of complexities because lower levels of converters exist.

THETA evolves organisms from lower to higher forms and supports them by the existence of lower converter forms.

Axiom 17: THETA, *via* LAMBDA, *effects an evolution of* MEST.

In this we have the waste products of organisms on the one hand as those very complex chemicals which bacteria make and, on the other hand, we have the physical face of the Earth being changed by animals and men, such changes as grass holding mountains from eroding or roots causing boulders to break, buildings being built and rivers being dammed. There is obviously an evolution in MEST in progress under the incursion[6] of THETA.

Axiom 18: LAMBDA, *even within a species, varies in its endowment of* THETA.

---

3. **harmonious:** agreeably related; in accord.

4. **thermal:** having to do with heat.

5. **intermediate:** being, situated or acting between two points.

6. **incursion:** a running, bringing or entering in or into, with vigorous, forceful or determined effort.

Axiom 19:   *The effort of* LAMBDA *is toward survival.*
    The goal of LAMBDA *is survival.*
    The penalty of failure to advance toward that goal is to
    succumb.
    DEFINITION: Persistence is the ability to exert con-
    tinuance of effort toward survival goals.

Axiom 20:   LAMBDA *creates, conserves, maintains, requires, de-*
    stroys, changes, occupies, groups and disperses MEST.
    LAMBDA *survives by animating and mobilizing or de-*
    stroying matter and energy in space and time.

Axiom 21:   LAMBDA *is dependent upon optimum motion. Motion*
    which is too swift and motion which is too slow are
    equally contrasurvival.

Axiom 22:   THETA *and thought are similar orders of static.*

Axiom 23:   *All thought is concerned with motion.*

Axiom 24:   *The establishment of an optimum motion is a basic*
    goal of reason.
    DEFINITION: LAMBDA is a chemical heat engine[7] exist-
    ing in space and time motivated by the life static
    and directed by thought.

Axiom 25:   *The basic purpose of reason is the calculation or esti-*
    mation of effort.

Axiom 26:   *Thought is accomplished by* THETA FACSIMILES[8] *of physi-*
    cal universe, entities or actions.

---

7. **chemical heat engine:** a mechanism for converting chemical energy (from food or
other fuel) into heat energy and mechanical energy; a body.

8. **facsimiles:** three-dimensional color pictures with sound and smell and all other
perceptions, plus the conclusions or speculations of the individual.

Axiom 27:   THETA *is satisfied only with harmonious action or optimum motion and rejects or destroys action or motion above or below its tolerance band.*

Axiom 28:   *The mind is concerned wholly with the estimation of effort.*
DEFINITION: Mind is the THETA command post of any organism or organisms.

Axiom 29:   *The basic errors of reason are failure to differentiate amongst matter, energy, space and time.*

Axiom 30:   *Rightness is proper calculation of effort.*

Axiom 31:   *Wrongness is always miscalculation of effort.*

Axiom 32:   THETA *can exert itself directly or extensionally.*
THETA can direct physical application of the organism to the environment or, through the mind, can first calculate the action or extend, as in language, ideas.

Axiom 33:   *Conclusions are directed toward the inhibition, maintenance or accelerations of efforts.*

Axiom 34:   *The common denominator of all life organisms is motion.*

Axiom 35:   *Effort of an organism to survive or succumb is physical motion of a life organism at a given moment in time through space.*
DEFINITION: Motion is any change in orientation[9] in space.
DEFINITION: Force is random effort.
DEFINITION: Effort is directed force.

---

9. **orientation:** alignment or position with respect to a reference system.

Axiom 36:   *An organism's effort can be to remain at rest or persist in a given motion.*

Static state has position in time, but an organism which is remaining positionally in a static state, if alive, is still continuing a highly complex pattern of motion, such as the heartbeat, digestion, etc.

The efforts of organisms to survive or succumb are assisted, compelled or opposed by the efforts of other organisms, matter, energy, space and time.

DEFINITION: Attention is a motion which must remain at an optimum effort.

Attention is aberrated by becoming unfixed and sweeping at random or becoming too fixed without sweeping.

Unknown threats to survival when sensed cause attention to sweep without fixing.

Known threats to survival when sensed cause attention to fix.

Axiom 37:   *The ultimate goal of* LAMBDA *is infinite survival.*

Axiom 38:   *Death is abandonment by* THETA *of a life organism or race or species where these can no longer serve* THETA *in its goals of infinite survival.*

Axiom 39:   *The reward of an organism engaging upon survival activity is pleasure.*

Axiom 40:   *The penalty of an organism failing to engage upon survival activity, or engaging in nonsurvival activity, is pain.*

Axiom 41:   *The cell and virus are the primary building blocks of life organisms.*

Axiom 42:   *The virus and cell are matter and energy animated and motivated in space and time by* THETA.

Axiom 43:   THETA *mobilizes the virus and cell in colonial aggregations[10] to increase potential motion and accomplish effort.*

Axiom 44:   *The goal of viruses and cells is survival in space through time.*

Axiom 45:   *The total mission of higher organisms, viruses and cells is the same as that of the virus and cell.*

Axiom 46:   *Colonial aggregations of viruses and cells can be imbued with more* THETA *than they inherently[11] contained.*

          Life energy joins any group, whether a group of organisms or group of cells composing an organism. Here we have personal entity, individuation,[12] etc.

Axiom 47:   *Effort can be accomplished by* LAMBDA *only through the coordination of its parts toward goals.*

Axiom 48:   *An organism is equipped to be governed and controlled by a mind.*

Axiom 49:   *The purpose of the mind is to pose and resolve problems relating to survival and to direct the effort of the organism according to these solutions.*

---

10. **aggregations:** masses formed by the union of distinct particles; gatherings, assemblages, collections.

11. **inherently:** in itself or oneself; by its or one's nature.

12. **individuation:** formation into an individual; development as a separate organic (living) unit.

Axiom 50:   *All problems are posed and resolved through estimations of effort.*

Axiom 51:   *The mind can confuse position in space with position in time. (Counter-efforts[13] producing action phrases.[14])*

Axiom 52:   *An organism proceeding toward survival is directed by the mind of that organism in the accomplishment of survival effort.*

Axiom 53:   *An organism proceeding toward succumb is directed by the mind of that organism in the accomplishment of death.*

Axiom 54:   *Survival of an organism is accomplished by the overcoming of efforts opposing its survival. (Note: Corollary for other dynamics.)*
DEFINITION: Dynamic is the ability to translate solutions into action.

Axiom 55:   *Survival effort for an organism includes the dynamic thrust by that organism for the survival of itself, its procreation, its group, its subspecies, its species, all life organisms, material universe, the life static and, possibly, a Supreme Being. (Note: List of dynamics.)*

Axiom 56:   *The cycle of an organism, a group of organisms or a species is inception,[15] growth, re-creation, decay and death.*

---

13. **counter-efforts:** the efforts of the environment (physical) against the individual. The individual's own effort is simply called effort. The efforts of the environment are called counter-efforts.

14. **action phrases:** words or phrases in engrams or locks which cause the individual to perform involuntary actions on the time track.

15. **inception:** beginning; start.

Axiom 57: The effort of an organism is directed toward the control of the environment for all the dynamics.

Axiom 58: Control of an environment is accomplished by the support of prosurvival factors along any dynamic.

Axiom 59: Any type of higher organism is accomplished by the evolution of viruses and cells into forms capable of better efforts to control or live in an environment.

Axiom 60: The usefulness of an organism is determined by its ability to control the environment or to support organisms which control the environment.

Axiom 61: An organism is rejected by THETA to the degree that it fails in its goals.

Axiom 62: Higher organisms can exist only in the degree that they are supported by the lower organisms.

Axiom 63: The usefulness of an organism is determined by the alignment of its efforts toward survival.

Axiom 64: The mind perceives and stores all data of the environment and aligns or fails to align these according to the time they were perceived.
DEFINITION: A conclusion is the THETA FACSIMILES of a group of combined data.
DEFINITION: A datum is a THETA FACSIMILE of physical action.

Axiom 65: The process of thought is the perception of the present and the comparison of it to the perceptions and conclusions of the past in order to direct action in the immediate or distant future.

COROLLARY: The attempt of thought is to perceive realities of the past and present in order to predict or postulate realities of the future.

Axiom 66: *The process by which life effects its conquest of the material universe consists in the conversion of the potential effort of matter and energy in space and through time to effect with it the conversion of further matter and energy in space and through time.*

Axiom 67: THETA *contains its own* THETA UNIVERSE *effort which translates into* MEST *effort.*

Axiom 68: *The single arbitrary in any organism is time.*

Axiom 69: *Physical universe perceptions and efforts are received by an organism as force waves, convert by facsimile into* THETA *and are thus stored.*
DEFINITION: Randomity is the misalignment through the internal or external efforts by other forms of life or the material universe of the efforts of an organism, and is imposed on the physical organism by counter-efforts in the environment.

Axiom 70: *Any cycle of any life organism is from static to motion to static.*

Axiom 71: *The cycle of randomity is from static, through optimum, through randomity sufficiently repetitious or similar to constitute another static.*

Axiom 72: *There are two subdivisions to randomity: data randomity and force randomity.*

Axiom 73: *The three degrees of randomity consist of minus randomity, optimum randomity and plus randomity.*
DEFINITION: Randomity is a component factor and necessary part of motion, if motion is to continue.

Axiom 74:   *Optimum randomity is necessary to learning.*

Axiom 75:   *The important factors in any area of randomity are effort and counter-effort. (Note: As distinguished from near perceptions of effort.)*

Axiom 76:   *Randomity amongst organisms is vital to continuous survival of all organisms.*

Axiom 77:   THETA *affects the organism, other organisms and the physical universe by translating* THETA FACSIMILES *into physical efforts or randomity of efforts.*
DEFINITION: The degree of randomity is measured by the randomness of effort vectors within the organism, amongst organisms, amongst races or species of organisms or between organisms and the physical universe.

Axiom 78:   *Randomity becomes intense in indirect ratio to the time in which it takes place, modified by the total effort in the area.*

Axiom 79:   *Initial randomity can be reinforced by randomities of greater or lesser magnitude.*

Axiom 80:   *Areas of randomity exist in chains of similarity plotted against time. This can be true of words and actions contained in randomities. Each may have its own chain plotted against time.*

Axiom 81:   *Sanity consists of optimum randomity.*

Axiom 82:   *Aberration exists to the degree that plus or minus randomity exists in the environment or past data of an organism, group or species, modified by the endowed self-determinism of that organism, group or species.*

Axiom 83: The self-determinism of an organism is determined by its THETA endowment, modified by minus or plus randomity in its environment or its existence.

Axiom 84: The self-determinism of an organism is increased by optimum randomity of counter-efforts.

Axiom 85: The self-determinism of an organism is reduced by plus or minus randomity of counter-efforts in the environment.

Axiom 86: Randomity contains both the randomness of efforts and the volume of efforts. (Note: An area of randomity can have a great deal of confusion, but without volume of energy, the confusion itself is negligible.[16])

Axiom 87: That counter-effort is most acceptable to an organism which most closely appears to assist its accomplishment of its goal.

Axiom 88: An area of severe plus or minus randomity can occlude[17] data on any of the subjects of that plus or minus randomity which took place in a prior time. (Note: Shut-off[18] mechanisms of earlier lives, perceptics,[19] specific incidents, etc.)

Axiom 89: Restimulation[20] of plus, minus or optimum randomity can produce increased plus, minus or optimum randomity respectively in the organism.

---

16. **negligible:** so small or unimportant that it may safely be neglected or disregarded.

17. **occlude:** hide; make unavailable to conscious recall.

18. **shut-off:** something that shuts off a flow or movement.

19. **perceptics:** sense messages.

20. **restimulation:** reactivation of a past memory due to similar circumstances in the present approximating circumstances of the past.

Axiom 90: An area of randomity can assume sufficient magnitude so as to appear to the organism as pain, according to its goals.

Axiom 91: Past randomity can impose itself upon the present organism as THETA FACSIMILES.

Axiom 92: The engram is a severe area of plus or minus randomity of sufficient volume to cause unconsciousness.

Axiom 93: Unconsciousness is an excess of randomity imposed by a counter-effort of sufficient force to cloud the awareness and direct function of the organism through the mind's control center.

Axiom 94: Any counter-effort which misaligns the organism's command of itself or its environment establishes plus or minus randomity or, if of sufficient magnitude, is an engram.

Axiom 95: Past engrams are restimulated by the control center's perception of circumstances similar to that engram in the present environment.

Axiom 96: An engram is a THETA FACSIMILE of atoms and molecules in misalignment.

Axiom 97: Engrams fix emotional response as that emotional response of the organism during the receipt of the counter-effort.

Axiom 98: Free emotional response depends on optimum randomity. It depends upon absence of or nonrestimulation of engrams.

Axiom 99: THETA FACSIMILES can recombine into new symbols.

Axiom 100: Language is the symbolization of effort.

Axiom 101: Language depends for its force upon the force which accompanied its definition. (Note: Counter-effort, not language, is aberrative.)

Axiom 102: The environment can occlude the central control of any organism and assume control of the motor[21] controls of that organism. (Engram, restimulation, locks,[22] hypnotism.)

Axiom 103: Intelligence depends on the ability to select aligned or misaligned data from an area of randomity and so discover a solution to reduce all randomity in that area.

Axiom 104: Persistence obtains in the ability of the mind to put solutions into physical action toward the realization of goals.

Axiom 105: An unknown datum can produce data of plus or minus randomity.

Axiom 106: The introduction of an arbitrary factor or force without recourse[23] to natural laws of the body or the area into which the arbitrary is introduced brings about plus or minus randomity.

Axiom 107: Data of plus or minus randomity depends for its confusion on former plus or minus randomity or absent data.

---

21. **motor:** causing or producing motion.

22. **locks:** mental image pictures of non-painful but disturbing experiences the person has experienced and which depend for their force on earlier secondaries and engrams which the experiences have restimulated (stirred up).

23. **recourse:** a turning or seeking for aid, safety, etc.

Axiom 108: Efforts which are inhibited or compelled by exterior efforts effect a plus or minus randomity of efforts.

Axiom 109: Behavior is modified by counter-efforts which have impinged on the organism.

Axiom 110: The component parts of THETA *are affinity, reality and communication.*

Axiom 111: Self-determinism consists of maximal[24] affinity, reality and communication.

Axiom 112: Affinity is the cohesion[25] of THETA.
Affinity manifests itself as the recognition of similarity of efforts and goals amongst organisms by those organisms.

Axiom 113: Reality is the agreement upon perceptions and data in the physical universe.
All that we can be sure is real is that on which we have agreed is real. Agreement is the essence of reality.

Axiom 114: Communication is the interchange of perception through the material universe between organisms or the perception of the material universe by sense channels.

Axiom 115: Self-determinism is the THETA *control of the organism.*

Axiom 116: A self-determined effort is that counter-effort which has been received into the organism in the past and integrated into the organism for its conscious use.

---

24. **maximal:** the highest or greatest possible.

25. **cohesion:** the force by which the molecules of a substance are held together: distinguished from adhesion. *See also* **adhesion** in the glossary.

Axiom 117: *The components of self-determinism are affinity, communication and reality.*
Self-determinism is manifested along each dynamic.

Axiom 118: *An organism cannot become aberrated unless it has agreed upon that aberration, has been in communication with a source of aberration and has had affinity for the aberrator.*

Axiom 119: *Agreement with any source, contra- or prosurvival, postulates a new reality for the organism.*

Axiom 120: *Nonsurvival courses, thoughts and actions require nonoptimum effort.*

Axiom 121: *Every thought has been preceded by physical action.*

Axiom 122: *The mind does with thought as it has done with entities in the physical universe.*

Axiom 123: *All effort concerned with pain is concerned with loss.*
Organisms hold pain and engrams to them as a latent[26] effort to prevent loss of some portion of the organism.
All loss is a loss of motion.

Axiom 124: *The amount of counter-effort the organism can overcome is proportional to the* THETA *endowment of the organism, modified by the physique[27] of that organism.*

Axiom 125: *Excessive counter-effort to the effort of a life organism produces unconsciousness.*

---

26. **latent:** not visible or apparent; hidden; dormant.
27. **physique:** physical or bodily structure, appearance or development.

COROLLARY: Unconsciousness gives the suppression of an organism's control center by counter-effort.

DEFINITION: The control center of the organism can be defined as the contact point between THETA and the physical universe and is that center which is aware of being aware and which has charge of and responsibility for the organism along all its dynamics.

Axiom 126: *Perceptions are always received in the control center of an organism whether the control center is in control of the organism at the time or not.*
This is an explanation for the assumption of valences.[28]

Axiom 127: *All perceptions reaching the organism's sense channels are recorded and stored by THETA FACSIMILE.*
DEFINITION: Perception is the process of recording data from the physical universe and storing it as a THETA FACSIMILE.
DEFINITION: Recall is the process of regaining perceptions.

Axiom 128: *Any organism can recall everything which it has perceived.*

Axiom 129: *An organism displaced by plus or minus randomity is thereafter remote from the perception recording center.*
Increased remoteness brings about occlusions of perceptions. One can perceive things in present

---

28. **valences:** personalities. The term is used to denote the borrowing of the personalities of others. Valences are substitutes for self taken on after the fact of lost confidence in self. Preclears "in their father's valence" are acting as though they were their father.

---

time and then, because they are being recorded after they passed THETA perception of the awareness unit, they are recorded but cannot be recalled.

Axiom 130: THETA FACSIMILES *of counter-effort are all that interpose[29] between the control center and its recalls.*

Axiom 131: *Any counter-effort received into a control center is always accompanied by all perceptics.*

Axiom 132: *The random counter-efforts to an organism and the intermingled perceptions in the randomity can reexert that force upon an organism when restimulated.*
DEFINITION: Restimulation is the reactivation of a past counter-effort by appearance in the organism's environment of a similarity toward the content of the past randomity area.

Axiom 133: *Self-determinism alone brings about the mechanism of restimulation.*

Axiom 134: *A reactivated area of the past randomity impinges the effort and the perceptions upon the organism.*

Axiom 135: *Activation of a randomity area is accomplished first by the perceptions, then by the pain, finally by the effort.*

Axiom 136: *The mind is plastically[30] capable of recording all efforts and counter-efforts.*

Axiom 137: *A counter-effort accompanied by sufficient (enrandomed) force impresses the facsimile of the counter-effort personality into the mind of an organism.*

---

29. **interpose:** to be or come between.
30. **plastically:** flexibly; impressionably.

Axiom 138: *Aberration is the degree of residual[31] plus or minus randomity accumulated by compelling, inhibiting or unwarranted[32] assisting of efforts on the part of other organisms or the physical (material) universe.*
Aberration is caused by what is done to the individual, not what the individual does, plus his self-determinism about what has been done to him.

Axiom 139: *Aberrated behavior consists of destructive effort toward prosurvival data or entities on any dynamic, or effort toward the survival of contrasurvival data or entities for any dynamic.*

Axiom 140: *A valence is a facsimile personality made capable of force by the counter-effort of the moment of receipt into the plus or minus randomity of unconsciousness.*
Valences are assistive, compulsive or inhibitive to the organism.
A control center is not a valence.

Axiom 141: *A control center effort is aligned toward a goal through definite space as a recognized incident in time.*

Axiom 142: *An organism is as healthy and sane as it is self-determined.*
The environmental control of the organism motor controls inhibits the organism's ability to change with the changing environment, since the organism will attempt to carry forward with one set of responses when it needs by self-determinism to create another to survive in another environment.

31. **residual:** remaining; left over.
32. **unwarranted:** not justified; unreasonable.

Axiom 143: *All learning is accomplished by random effort.*

Axiom 144: *A counter-effort producing sufficient plus or minus randomity to record is recorded with an index of space and time as hidden as the remainder of its content.*

Axiom 145: *A counter-effort producing sufficient plus or minus randomity when activated by restimulation exerts itself against the environment or the organism without regard to space and time, except reactivated perceptions.*

Axiom 146: *Counter-efforts are directed out from the organism until they are further enrandomed by the environ at which time they again activate against the control center.*

Axiom 147: *An organism's mind employs counter-efforts effectively only so long as insufficient plus or minus randomity exists to hide differentiation of the facsimiles created.*

Axiom 148: *Physical laws are learned by life energy only by impingement of the physical universe producing randomity, and a withdrawal from that impingement.*

Axiom 149: *Life depends upon an alignment of force vectors in the direction of survival and the nullification of force vectors in the direction of succumb in order to survive.*
COROLLARY: Life depends upon an alignment of force vectors in the direction of succumb and the nullification of force vectors in the direction of survive in order to succumb.

Axiom 150: *Any area of randomity gathers to it situations similar to it which do not contain actual efforts but only perceptions.*

Axiom 151: Whether an organism has the goal of surviving or succumbing depends upon the amount of plus or minus randomity it has reactivated. *(Not residual.)*

Axiom 152: Survival is accomplished only by motion.

Axiom 153: In the physical universe the absence of motion is vanishment.

Axiom 154: Death is the equivalent to life of total lack of life-motivated motion.

Axiom 155: Acquisition of prosurvival matter and energy or organisms in space and time means increased motion.

Axiom 156: Loss of prosurvival matter and energy or organisms in space and time means decreased motion.

Axiom 157: Acquisition or proximity[33] of matter, energy or organisms which assist the survival of an organism increase the survival potentials of an organism.

Axiom 158: Acquisition or proximity of matter, energy or organisms which inhibit the survival of an organism decrease its survival potential.

Axiom 159: Gain of survival energy, matter or organisms increases the freedom of an organism.

Axiom 160: Receipt or proximity of nonsurvival energy, matter or time decreases the freedom of motion of an organism.

Axiom 161: The control center attempts the halting or lengthening of time, the expansion or contraction of space and the decrease or increase of energy and matter.

---

33. **proximity:** nearness.

This is a primary source of invalidation, and it is also a primary source of aberration.

Axiom 162: *Pain is the balk of effort by counter-effort in great intensity, whether that effort is to remain at rest or in motion.*

Axiom 163: *Perception, including pain, can be exhausted from an area of plus or minus randomity, still leaving the effort and counter-effort of that plus or minus randomity.*

Axiom 164: *The rationality of the mind depends upon an optimum reaction toward time.*
DEFINITION: Sanity, the computation of futures.
DEFINITION: Neurotic, the computation of present time only.
DEFINITION: Psychotic, computation only of past situations.

Axiom 165: *Survival pertains only to the future.*
COROLLARY: Succumb pertains only to the present and past.

Axiom 166: *An individual is as happy as he can perceive survival potentials in the future.*

Axiom 167: *As the needs of any organism are met it rises higher and higher in its efforts along the dynamics.*
An organism which achieves ARC with itself can better achieve ARC with sex in the future; having achieved this it can achieve ARC with groups; having achieved this, it can achieve ARC with mankind, etc.

Axiom 168: *Affinity, reality and communication coexist in an inextricable relationship.*

The coexistent relationship between affinity, reality and communication is such that none can be increased without increasing the other two and none can be decreased without decreasing the other two.

Axiom 169: *Any aesthetic[34] product is a symbolic facsimile or combination of facsimiles of* THETA *or physical universes in varied randomities and volumes of randomities with the interplay of tones.*

Axiom 170: *An aesthetic product is an interpretation of the universes by an individual or group mind.*

Axiom 171: *Delusion is the postulation by the imagination of occurrences in areas of plus or minus randomity.*

Axiom 172: *Dreams are the imaginative reconstruction of areas of randomity or the resymbolization of the efforts of* THETA.

Axiom 173: *A motion is created by the degree of optimum randomity introduced by the counter-effort to an organism's effort.*

Axiom 174: *MEST which has been mobilized by life forms is in more affinity with life organisms than nonmobilized* MEST.

Axiom 175: *All past perception, conclusion and existence moments, including those of plus or minus randomity, are recoverable to the control center of the organism.*

---

34. **aesthetic:** having the nature of a wavelength closely resembling theta or a harmony approximating theta; beautiful.

Axiom 176: The ability to produce survival effort on the part of an organism is affected by the degrees of randomity existing in its past. (This includes learning.)

Axiom 177: Areas of past plus or minus randomity can be readdressed by the control center of an organism and the plus or minus randomity exhausted.

Axiom 178: The exhaustion of past plus or minus randomities permits the control center of an organism to effect its own efforts toward survival goals.

Axiom 179: The exhaustion of self-determined effort from a past area of plus or minus randomity nullifies the effectiveness of that area.

Axiom 180: Pain is the randomity produced by sudden or strong counter-efforts.

Axiom 181: Pain is stored as plus or minus randomity.

Axiom 182: Pain, as an area of plus or minus randomity, can reinflict itself upon the organism.

Axiom 183: Past pain becomes ineffective upon the organism when the randomity of its area is addressed and aligned.

Axiom 184: The earlier the area of plus or minus randomity, the greater self-produced effort existed to repel it.

Axiom 185: Later areas of plus or minus randomity cannot be realigned easily until earlier areas are realigned.

Axiom 186: Areas of plus or minus randomity become increased in activity when perceptions of similarity are introduced into them.

Axiom 187: *Past areas of plus or minus randomity can be reduced and aligned by address to them in present time.*

Axiom 188: *Absolute good and absolute evil do not exist in the* MEST *universe.*

Axiom 189: *That which is good for an organism may be defined as that which promotes the survival of that organism.*
COROLLARY: Evil may be defined as that which inhibits or brings plus or minus randomity into the organism, which is contrary to the survival motives of the organism.

Axiom 190: *Happiness consists in the act of bringing alignment into hitherto resisting plus or minus randomity. Neither the act or action of attaining survival, nor the accomplishment of this act itself, brings about happiness.*

Axiom 191: *Construction is an alignment of data.*
COROLLARY: Destruction is a plus or minus randomity of data.
The effort of constructing is the alignment toward the survival of the aligning organism.
Destruction is the effort of bringing randomity into an area.

Axiom 192: *Optimum survival behavior consists of effort in the maximum survival interest in everything concerned in the dynamics.*

Axiom 193: *The optimum survival solution of any problem would consist of the highest attainable survival for every dynamic concerned.*

Axiom 194: *The worth of any organism consists of its value to the survival of its own* THETA *along any dynamic.*

6

The Prelogics and Scientology Axioms

The Qs
(Prelogics)

[1952]

Knowledge is a pyramid, and knowledge as a pyramid has a common denominator which evaluates all other data below it. At the top point of this pyramid, we have what could be called a Q, and it could also be called a common denominator. It is in common to every other datum in this pyramid full of data.

The Qs are the highest echelon from which all other things are derived.

Q came from *quod* in Q.E.D. (*quod erat demonstrandum*, meaning "which was to be shown or demonstrated," used especially in mathematical proofs).

Actually, Q can be defined this way: It is the level from which we are now viewing, which is a common denominator to all experience which we can now view. This is the level which acts as a common denominator to all this experience, and is the highest level from which we are operating. This data, then, would stand behind everything else that we do.

Q simply means the most common datum that sums all other data.

Q 1:   *Self-determinism is the common denominator of all life impulses.*

Q 2:   *Definition of self-determinism: the ability to locate in space and time, energy and matter, also the ability to create space and time in which to create and locate energy and matter.*

Q 3:   *The identification of the source of that which places matter and energy and originates space and time is not necessary to the resolution of this problem at this time.*

Q 4:   *Theta creates space, energy and objects by postulates.*

Q 5:   *Universes are created by the application of self-determinism on eight dynamics.*

Q 6:   *Self-determinism, applied, will create, alter, conserve and possibly destroy universes.*

Q 7:   *The action cycle is one of the abilities of a thetan. An action cycle goes from 40.0^1 to 0.0^2 on the Tone Scale.[3] An action cycle is the creation, growth, conservation, decay and death or destruction of energy and matter in a space. Action cycles produce time.*

---

1. **40.0:** *see* **Tone Scale in Full** in the Scales section of this book.

2. **0.0:** *see* **Tone Scale in Full** in the Scales section of this book.

3. **Tone Scale:** a gradient scale which plots the descending spiral of life from full vitality and consciousness through half-vitality and half-consciousness down to death and the minus tones lying beneath death on the scale. *See also* **Tone Scale in Full** in the Scales section of this book.

The Axioms
of Scientology

[1954]

Axiom 1: *Life is basically a static.*
DEFINITION: A life static has no mass, no motion, no wavelength, no location in space or in time. It has the ability to postulate and to perceive.

Axiom 2: *The static is capable of considerations, postulates and opinions.*

Axiom 3: *Space, energy, objects, form and time are the result of considerations made and/or agreed upon by the static and are perceived solely because the static considers that it can perceive them.*

Axiom 4: *Space is a viewpoint[1] of dimension.[2]*

Axiom 5: *Energy consists of postulated particles in space.*

Axiom 6: *Objects consist of grouped particles.*

---

1. **viewpoint:** a point of awareness from which one can perceive.

2. **dimension:** the distance from the point of view to the anchor point that is in space; a measure of spatial extent, especially width, height or length.

Axiom 7: Time is basically a postulate that space and particles will persist.

Axiom 8: The apparency[3] of time is the change of position of particles in space.

Axiom 9: Change is the primary manifestation of time.

Axiom 10: The highest purpose in the universe is the creation of an effect.

Axiom 11: The considerations resulting in conditions of existence are fourfold:

(a) As-isness is the condition of immediate creation without persistence, and is the condition of existence which exists at the moment of creation and the moment of destruction, and is different from other considerations in that it does not contain survival.

(b) Alter-isness is the consideration which introduces change, and therefore time and persistence, into an as-isness to obtain persistency.

(c) Isness is an apparency of existence brought about by the continuous alteration of an as-isness. This is called, when agreed upon, reality.

(d) Not-isness is the effort to handle isness by reducing its condition through the use of force. It is an apparency and cannot entirely vanquish[4] an isness.

Axiom 12: The primary condition of any universe is that two spaces, energies or objects must not occupy the same

3. **apparency:** that which appears to be, as distinct from what actually is.
4. **vanquish:** overcome.

space. When this condition is violated (a perfect duplicate) the apparency of any universe or any part thereof is nulled.

Axiom 13: The cycle of action of the physical universe is create, survive (which is persist), destroy.

Axiom 14: Survival is accomplished by alter-isness and not-isness, by which is gained the persistency known as time.

Axiom 15: Creation is accomplished by the postulation of an as-isness.

Axiom 16: Complete destruction is accomplished by the postulation of the as-isness of any existence and the parts thereof.

Axiom 17: The static, having postulated as-isness, then practices alter-isness, and so achieves the apparency of isness and so obtains reality.

Axiom 18: The static, in practicing not-isness, brings about the persistence of unwanted existences, and so brings about unreality, which includes forgetfulness, unconsciousness and other undesirable states.

Axiom 19: Bringing the static to view as-is any condition devaluates that condition.

Axiom 20: Bringing the static to create a perfect duplicate causes the vanishment of any existence or part thereof.
A perfect duplicate is an additional creation of the object, its energy and space, in its own space, in its own time using its own energy. This violates the condition that two objects must not occupy the same space, and causes the vanishment of the object.

Axiom 21: *Understanding is composed of affinity, reality and communication.*

Axiom 22: *The practice of not-isness reduces understanding.*

Axiom 23: *The static has the capability of total knowingness. Total knowingness would consist of total ARC.*

Axiom 24: *Total ARC would bring about the vanishment of all mechanical conditions of existence.*

Axiom 25: *Affinity is a scale of attitudes which falls away from the coexistence of static, through the interpositions of distance and energy, to create identity, down to close proximity but mystery.*

By the practice of isness (beingness) and not-isness (refusal to be) individuation[5] progresses from the knowingness of complete identification down through the introduction of more and more distance and less and less duplication, through lookingness, emotingness,[6] effortingness, thinkingness, symbolizingness, eatingness, sexingness, and so through to not-knowingness (mystery). Until the point of mystery is reached, some communication is possible, but even at mystery an attempt to communicate continues. Here we have, in the case of an individual, a gradual falling away from the belief that one can assume a complete affinity down to the conviction that all is a complete mystery. Any individual is somewhere on this Know to Mystery Scale. The original Chart of Human Evaluation was the emotion section of this scale.

---

5. **individuation:** a withdrawal out of groups and into only self. The mechanics of individuation are first, communication into, and then refusal to communicate into.

6. **emotingness:** the condition of having or manifesting emotion.

Axiom 26: Reality is the agreed-upon apparency of existence.

*Axiom 27: An actuality can exist for one individually, but when it
is agreed with by others it can be said to be a reality.*
The anatomy of reality is contained in isness, which
is composed of as-isness and alter-isness. An isness
is an apparency, not an actuality. The actuality is
as-isness altered so as to obtain a persistency.
Unreality is the consequence and apparency of the
practice of not-isness.

*Axiom 28: Communication is the consideration and action of impel-
ling an impulse or particle from source-point across a
distance to receipt-point, with the intention of bringing
into being at the receipt-point a duplication and understanding of that which emanated from the source-point.*
The formula[7] of communication is: cause, distance,
effect, with intention, attention and duplication with
understanding.
The component parts of communication are consideration, intention, attention, cause, source-point,
distance, effect, receipt-point, duplication, understanding, the velocity of the impulse or particle,
nothingness or somethingness.
A noncommunication consists of barriers. Barriers
consist of space, interpositions (such as walls and
screens of fast-moving particles) and time. A communication, by definition, does not need to be two-
way. When a communication is returned, the formula
is repeated, with the receipt-point now becoming
a source-point and the former source-point now
becoming a receipt-point.

---

7. **formula:** a rule or method for doing something.

Axiom 29: In order to cause an as-isness to persist, one must assign other authorship to the creation than his own. Otherwise, his view of it would cause its vanishment.

Any space, energy, form, object, individual or physical universe condition can exist only when an alteration has occurred of the original as-isness so as to prevent a casual view from vanishing it. In other words, anything which is persisting must contain a "lie" so that the original consideration is not completely duplicated.

Axiom 30: The general rule of auditing is that anything which is unwanted and yet persists must be thoroughly viewed, at which time it will vanish.

If only partially viewed, its intensity, at least, will decrease.

Axiom 31: Goodness and badness, beautifulness and ugliness are alike considerations and have no other basis than opinion.

Axiom 32: Anything which is not directly observed tends to persist.

Axiom 33: Any as-isness which is altered by not-isness (by force) tends to persist.

Axiom 34: Any isness, when altered by force, tends to persist.

Axiom 35: The ultimate truth is a static.

A static has no mass, meaning, mobility, no wavelength, no time, no location in space, no space.

This has the technical name of "basic truth."

Axiom 36: A lie is a second postulate, statement or condition designed to mask a primary postulate which is permitted to remain.

EXAMPLES:

Neither truth nor a lie is a motion or alteration of a particle from one position to another.

A lie is a statement that a particle having moved did not move, or a statement that a particle, not having moved, did move.

The basic lie is that a consideration which was made was not made or that it was different.

Axiom 37: *When a primary consideration is altered but still exists, persistence is achieved for the altering consideration.*

All persistence depends on the basic truth, but the persistence is of the altering consideration, for the basic truth has neither persistence nor impersistence.

Axiom 38: 1. *Stupidity is the unknownness of consideration.*

2. *Mechanical definition: Stupidity is the unknownness of time, place, form and event.*

1. *Truth is the exact consideration.*

2. *Truth is the exact time, place, form and event.*

Thus we see that failure to discover truth brings about stupidity.

Thus we see that the discovery of truth would bring about an as-isness by actual experiment.

Thus we see that an ultimate truth would have no time, place, form or event. Thus, then, we perceive that we can achieve a persistence only when we mask a truth.

Lying is an alteration of time, place, event or form.

Lying becomes alter-isness, becomes stupidity.

(The blackness of cases[8] is an accumulation of the case's own or another's lies.)

---

8. **cases:** a general term for people being treated or helped. It also refers to their condition, which is monitored by the content of the reactive mind. A person's case is the way he responds to the world around him by reason of his aberrations.

Anything which persists must avoid as-isness. Thus, anything, to persist, must contain a lie.

Axiom 39: *Life poses problems for its own solution.*

Axiom 40: *Any problem, to be a problem, must contain a lie. If it were truth, it would unmock.*[9]
An "unsolvable problem" would have the greatest persistence. It would also contain the greatest number of altered facts. To make a problem, one must introduce alter-isness.

Axiom 41: *That into which alter-isness is introduced becomes a problem.*

Axiom 42: *Matter, energy, space and time persists because it is a problem.*
It is a problem because it contains alter-isness.

Axiom 43: *Time is the primary source of untruth.*
Time states the untruth of consecutive considerations.

Axiom 44: *Theta, the static, has no location in matter, energy, space or time, but is capable of consideration.*

Axiom 45: *Theta can consider itself to be placed, at which moment it becomes placed, and to that degree a problem.*

Axiom 46: *Theta can become a problem by its considerations, but then becomes* MEST.
MEST *is that form of theta which is a problem.*

Axiom 47: *Theta can resolve problems.*

---

9. **unmock:** become nothing.

Axiom 48: Life is a game wherein theta as the static solves the problems of theta as MEST.

Axiom 49: To solve any problem it is only necessary to become theta, the solver, rather than theta, the problem.

Axiom 50: Theta as MEST must contain considerations which are lies.

Axiom 51: Postulates and live communication not being MEST and being senior to MEST can accomplish change in MEST without bringing about a persistence of MEST. Thus auditing can occur.

Axiom 52: MEST persists and solidifies to the degree that it is not granted life.

Axiom 53: A stable datum is necessary to the alignment of data.

Axiom 54: A tolerance of confusion and an agreed-upon stable datum on which to align the data in a confusion are at once necessary for a sane reaction on the eight dynamics. (This defines sanity.)

Axiom 55: The cycle of action is a consideration. Create, survive, destroy, the cycle of action accepted by the GE,[10] is only a consideration which can be changed by the thetan, making a new consideration or different action cycles.

---

10. **GE:** the genetic entity. It is that beingness not dissimilar to the thetan that has carried forward and developed the body from its earliest moments along the evolutionary line on Earth and which, through experience, necessity and natural selection, has employed the counter-efforts of the environment to fashion an organism of the type best fitted for survival, limited only by the abilities of the GE. The goal of the GE is survival on a much grosser plane of materiality (concerning the material or physical).

Axiom 56: Theta brings order to chaos.
           COROLLARY: Chaos brings disorder to theta.

Axiom 57: Order manifests when communication, control and havingness are available to theta.
           DEFINITIONS: Communication: the interchange of ideas across space.
           Control: positive postulating, which is intention, and the execution thereof.
           Havingness: that which permits the experience of mass and pressure.

Axiom 58: Intelligence and judgment are measured by the ability to evaluate relative importances.
           COROLLARY: The ability to evaluate importances and unimportances is the highest faculty of logic.
           COROLLARY: Identification is a monotone assignment of importance.
           COROLLARY: Identification is the inability to evaluate differences in time, location, form, composition or importance.

The above is a summary of states of being which can be used to create, cause to persist, or destroy.

Having agreed to the mechanics and retaining the agreements, the thetan can yet make innumerable postulates which by their contradiction and complexity, create, cause to persist, and destroy human behavior.

The Axioms and Formulas of SOP 8-C

[1954]

I: LOCATION

PRELOGIC: *Theta orients objects in space and time.*

AXIOM: *In life experience space becomes beingness.*

FORMULA I: *Permitting the preclear[1] to discover with certainty where people and things are not in the present, past and future recovers sufficient orientation to establish his knowledge and certainty of where he is and they are; the application of this is accomplished by negative orientation of beingness, havingness and doingness on each of eight dynamics in the present, past and future.*

II: BODIES

AXIOM: *In life experience energy becomes doingness.*

AXIOM: *Compulsive position precedes compulsive thinking.*

AXIOM: *That which changes the preclear in space can evaluate for him.*

FORMULA II: *Permit the preclear to discover that he handles bodies and allow him to handle bodies in mock-ups and actuality; and remedy his thirst for attention which he has received by contagion from bodies.*

---

1. **preclear:** a spiritual being who is now on the road to becoming Clear, hence pre-Clear.

III: SPACE

PRELOGIC: *Theta creates space and time and objects to locate in them.*

DEFINITION: *Space is a viewpoint of dimension.*

AXIOM: *Energy derives from imposition of space between terminals[2] and a reduction and expansion of that space.*

FORMULA III: *Permit the preclear to regain his ability to create space and impose it upon terminals, to remove it from between terminals and to regain his security concerning the stability of MEST space.*

IV: HAVINGNESS

AXIOM: *In life experience matter becomes havingness.*

OBSERVATION: *To a thetan, anything is better than nothing.*

OBSERVATION: *Any preclear is suffering from problems of too little havingness and any reduction of his existing energy, if not replaced, will cause him to drop in tone.*

FORMULA IV:

a. *The remedy of problems of havingness is accomplished by creating an abundance of all things.*

b. *As the preclear has rendered automatic his desires and ability to create and destroy, and has thus placed havingness beyond his control, the auditor should place in the control of the preclear his automaticities of havingness and unhavingness and permit him, on his own self-determinism, to balance his havingness.*

c. *How to make havingness: Have preclear put out eight anchor points[3] of size, thus creating a space. Have him*

---

2. **terminals:** things that can receive, relay or send communications (most common usage); also, things with mass and meaning.

3. **anchor points:** dimension points which demark the outermost boundaries of a space or its corners. Anchor points, along with the viewpoint, are responsible for space. An anchor point is a dimension point that stays rather still, to keep the space created.

pull in these eight to the center and have him retain the resulting mass. Do this using large and various objects for anchor points. Do this until he is willing to release such old energy deposits as engrams and ridges but still continue to make havingness.

V: TERMINALS

AXIOM: *Space exists by reason of anchor points.*

DEFINITION: *An anchor point is any particle or mass or terminal.*

AXIOM: *Energy is derived from mass by fixing two terminals in proximity in space.*

AXIOM: *Self-determinism is related to the ability to impose space between terminals.*

AXIOM: *Cause is a potential source of flow.*[4]

AXIOM: *Effect is a potential receipt of flow.*

AXIOM: *Communication is the duplication of the receipt-point of that which emanated at a cause-point.*

AXIOM: *Wrongness in terms of flow is inflow.*

FORMULA V: *The thetan is rehabilitated*[5] *as to energy and terminals by remedying his postulates about outflow and inflow and drills relating to the outflow and inflow of energy according to the above axioms.*

VI: SYMBOLIZATION

DEFINITION: *A symbol is an idea fixed in energy and mobile in space.*

FORMULA VI: *The thetan who has been moved about by symbols is strengthened by mocking up and moving about and fixing in space ideas which have formerly moved him.*

---

4. **flow:** a directional thought, energy or action.

5. **rehabilitated:** restored to some former ability or state of being or some more optimum condition.

VII: BARRIERS

AXIOM: *The* MEST *universe is a game consisting of barriers.*

DEFINITION: *A barrier is space, energy, object obstacles or time.*

FORMULA VII: *Problems of barriers or their lack are resolved by contacting and penetrating, creating and destroying, validating and neglecting barriers by changing them or substituting others for them, by fixing and unfixing attention upon their somethingness and nothingness.*

VIII: DUPLICATION

FUNDAMENTAL: *The basic action of existence is duplication.*

LOGIC: *All operating principles of life may be derived from duplication.*

AXIOM: *Communication is as exact as it approaches duplication.*

AXIOM: *Unwillingness to be cause is monitored by unwillingness to be duplicated.*

AXIOM: *Unwillingness to be an effect is monitored by unwillingness to duplicate.*

AXIOM: *An inability to remain in a geographical position brings about an unwillingness to duplicate.*

AXIOM: *An enforced fixation in a geographical position brings about an unwillingness to duplicate.*

AXIOM: *Inability to duplicate on any dynamic is the primary degeneration of the thetan.*

AXIOM: *Perception depends upon duplication.*

AXIOM: *Communication depends upon duplication.*

AXIOM: *In the* MEST *universe, the single crime is duplication.*

FORMULA VIII: *The primary ability and willingness of the thetan to duplicate must be rehabilitated by handling desires, enforcements and inhibitions relating to it on all dynamics.*

7

The Factors

7

The Factors

[1953]

(Summation of the considerations and examinations of the human spirit and the material universe completed between 1923 and 1953 A.D.)

1. Before the beginning was a Cause and the entire purpose of the Cause was the creation of effect.

2. In the beginning and forever is the decision and the decision is TO BE.

3. The first action of beingness is to assume a viewpoint.

4. The second action of beingness is to extend from the viewpoint, points to view, which are dimension points.

5. Thus there is space created, for the definition of space is: viewpoint of dimension. And the purpose of a dimension point is space and a point of view.

6. The action of a dimension point is reaching and withdrawing.

7. And from the viewpoint to the dimension points there are connection and interchange. Thus new dimension points are made. Thus there is communication.

8. And thus there is light.

9. And thus there is energy.

10. And thus there is life.

11. But there are other viewpoints and these viewpoints outthrust points to view. And there comes about an interchange amongst viewpoints; but the interchange is never otherwise than in terms of exchanging dimension points.

12. The dimension point can be moved by the viewpoint, for the viewpoint, in addition to creative ability and consideration, possesses volition and potential independence of action; and the viewpoint, viewing dimension points, can change in relation to its own or other dimension points or viewpoints. Thus comes about all the fundamentals there are to motion.

13. The dimension points are each and every one, whether large or small, *solid*. And they are solid solely because the viewpoints say they are solid.

14. Many dimension points combine into larger gases, fluids or solids. Thus there is matter. But the most valued point is admiration, and admiration is so strong its absence alone permits persistence.

15. The dimension point can be different from other dimension points and thus can possess an individual

quality. And many dimension points can possess a similar quality, and others can possess a similar quality unto[1] themselves. Thus comes about the quality of classes of matter.

16. The viewpoint can combine dimension points into forms and the forms can be simple or complex and can be at different distances from the viewpoints and so there can be combinations of form. And the forms are capable of motion and the viewpoints are capable of motion and so there can be motion of forms.

17. And the opinion of the viewpoint regulates the consideration of the forms, their stillness or their motion, and these considerations consist of assignment of beauty or ugliness to the forms and these considerations alone are art.

18. It is the opinions of the viewpoints that some of these forms should endure. Thus there is survival.

19. And the viewpoint can never perish; but the form can perish.

20. And the many viewpoints, interacting, become dependent upon one another's forms and do not choose to distinguish completely the ownership of dimension points and so comes about a dependency upon the dimension points and upon the other viewpoints.

21. From this comes a consistency of viewpoint of the interaction of dimension points and this, regulated, is TIME.

---

1. **unto:** a compound of *un* (on) and *to*. It is simply an obsolete form of "to," and is mainly used as a poetic device or for effect.

22. And there are universes.

23. The universes, then, are three in number: the universe created by one viewpoint, the universe created by every other viewpoint, the universe created by the mutual action of viewpoints which is agreed to be upheld—the physical universe.

24. And the viewpoints are never seen. And the viewpoints consider more and more that the dimension points are valuable. And the viewpoints try to become the anchor points and forget that they can create more points and space and forms. Thus comes about scarcity. And the dimension points can perish and so the viewpoints assume that they, too, can perish.

25. Thus comes about death.

26. The manifestations of pleasure and pain, of thought, emotion and effort, of thinking, of sensation, of affinity, reality, communication, of behavior and being are thus derived and the riddles of our universe are apparently contained and answered herein.

27. There *is* beingness, but man believes there is only becomingness.

28. The resolution of any problem posed hereby is the establishment of viewpoints and dimension points, the betterment of condition and concourse amongst dimension points, and, thereby, viewpoints, and the remedy of abundance or scarcity in all things, pleasant or ugly, by the rehabilitation of the ability of the viewpoint to assume points of view and create and uncreate, neglect, start, change and stop dimension points

of any kind at the determinism of the viewpoint. Certainty in all three universes must be regained, for certainty, not data, is knowledge.

29. In the opinion of the viewpoint, any beingness, any thing, is better than no thing, any effect is better than no effect, any universe better than no universe, any particle better than no particle, but the particle of admiration is best of all.

30. And above these things there might be speculation only. And below these things there is the playing of the game. But these things which are written here man can experience and know. And some may care to teach these things and some may care to use them to assist those in distress and some may desire to employ them to make individuals and organizations more able and so give to Earth a culture of which we can be proud.

Humbly tendered as a gift to man
by L. Ron Hubbard, 23 April 1953

8

Scales

Gradient Scales

The term "gradient scale" can be applied to anything, and means a scale of condition graduated from zero to infinity.

Absolutes are considered unobtainable.

Depending on the direction in which the scale is graduated, there could be an infinity of wrongness or an infinity of rightness. Thus the gradient scale of rightness would run from the theoretical but unobtainable zero of rightness, up to the theoretical infinity of rightness. A gradient scale of wrongness would run from a zero of wrongness to an infinity of wrongness. This is called "infinity-valued logic."

Gradient Scale of the Relative Value of Data

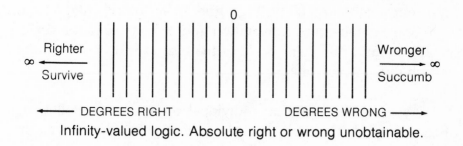

Infinity-valued logic. Absolute right or wrong unobtainable.

The word "gradient" is meant to define lessening or increasing degrees of condition.

The difference between one point on these scales and another point could be as different or as wide as the entire range of the scale itself, or it could be so tiny as to need the most minute discernment for its establishment.

Terms like good and bad, alive and dead, right and wrong, are used only in conjunction with gradient scales.

The gradient scale is a way of thinking about the universe which approximates the actual conditions of the universe more closely than any other existing logical method.

Life in its highest state (top of the scale) is *understanding.* Life in its lower states is in a lower level of understanding.

Understanding is composed of affinity, reality and communication. This triangle tells us that the coexistent relationship between affinity, reality and communication is such that none can be increased without a resulting increase in the other two and none can be decreased without decreasing the other two. Of the three, *communication* is by far the most important. Affinity and reality exist to further communication. Under the heading of affinity we have, for instance, all the varied emotions which go from apathy at 0.05 through grief, fear, anger, antagonism, boredom, enthusiasm, exhilaration and serenity *in that order.* It is affinity and this rising scale of the characteristics of emotion which give us the Tone Scale.

Wherever you find an individual on any of the following scales, that is his level of ARC. As a person goes upscale in auditing, he goes upscale on gradients of ARC.

Tone Scale
[1950]

Tone Scale

4.0	Eagerness, Exhilaration
3.5	Strong Interest
3.0	Conservatism
2.5	Boredom
2.0	Antagonism (Overt Hostility)
1.5	Anger
1.1	Covert Hostility
1.0	Fear
0.5	Grief
0.2	Apathy
0.0	Death

Tone Scale Expanded

[1978]

Tone Scale

40.0	Serenity of Beingness
30.0	Postulates
22.0	Games
20.0	Action
8.0	Exhilaration
6.0	Aesthetic
4.0	Enthusiasm
3.5	Cheerfulness
3.3	Strong Interest
3.0	Conservatism
2.9	Mild Interest
2.8	Contented
2.6	Disinterested
2.5	Boredom
2.4	Monotony
2.0	Antagonism
1.9	Hostility
1.8	Pain
1.5	Anger
1.4	Hate
1.3	Resentment
1.2	No Sympathy
1.15	Unexpressed Resentment
1.1	Covert Hostility
1.02	Anxiety
1.0	Fear
.98	Despair
.96	Terror
.94	Numb
.9	Sympathy

(continued on next page)

Tone Scale

.8	Propitiation (Higher Toned— Selectively Gives)
.5	Grief
.375	Making Amends (Propitiation— Can't Withhold Anything)
.3	Undeserving
.2	Self-Abasement[1]
.1	Victim
.07	Hopeless
.05	Apathy
.03	Useless
.01	Dying
0.0	Body Death
−0.01	Failure
−0.1	Pity
−0.2	Shame (Being Other Bodies)
−0.7	Accountable
−1.0	Blame (Punishing Bodies)
−1.3	Regret (Responsibility as Blame)
−1.5	Controlling Bodies
−2.2	Protecting Bodies
−3.0	Owning Bodies
−3.5	Approval from Bodies
−4.0	Needing Bodies
−5.0	Worshiping Bodies
−6.0	Sacrifice
−8.0	Hiding
−10.0	Being Objects
−20.0	Being Nothing
−30.0	Can't Hide
−40.0	Total Failure

---

1. **self-abasement:** a lowering, humiliating or degrading of oneself.

Tone Scale in Full

[1978]

Tone Scale Expanded	Tone Scale	Know to Mystery Scale
Serenity of Beingness	40.0	Know
Postulates	30.0	Not Know
Games	22.0	Know About
Action	20.0	Look
Exhilaration	8.0	Plus Emotion
Aesthetic	6.0	
Enthusiasm	4.0	
Cheerfulness	3.5	
Strong Interest	3.3	
Conservatism	3.0	
Mild Interest	2.9	
Contented	2.8	
Disinterested	2.6	
Boredom	2.5	
Monotony	2.4	
Antagonism	2.0	Minus
Hostility	1.9	Emotion
Pain	1.8	
Anger	1.5	
Hate	1.4	
Resentment	1.3	
No Sympathy	1.2	
Unexpressed Resentment	1.15	
Covert Hostility	1.1	
Anxiety	1.02	
Fear	1.0	
Despair	.98	
Terror	.96	
Numb	.94	
Sympathy	.9	
Propitiation	.8	
(Higher toned— Selectively Gives)		

THETAN SCALE RANGE
Extends well below body death at "0" down to complete unbeingness as a thetan

THETAN PLUS BODY
Social training and education sole guarantee of sane conduct

(continued on next page)

	Tone Scale Expanded	Tone Scale	Know to Mystery Scale
THETAN PLUS BODY Social training and education sole guarantee of sane conduct	Grief	.5	
	Making Amends (Propitiation—Can't Withhold Anything)	.375	
	Undeserving	.3	
	Self-Abasement	.2	
	Victim	.1	
	Hopeless	.07	
	Apathy	.05	
	Useless	.03	
	Dying	.01	
	Body Death	0.0	
THETAN SCALE RANGE Extends well below body death at "0" down to complete unbeingness as a thetan	Failure	−0.01	
	Pity	−0.1	
	Shame	−0.2	
	(Being Other Bodies)		
	Accountable	−0.7	
	Blame	−1.0	
	(Punishing Bodies)		
	Regret	−1.3	
	(Responsibility as Blame)		
	Controlling Bodies	−1.5	Effort
	Protecting Bodies	−2.2	
	Owning Bodies	−3.0	Think
	Approval from Bodies	−3.5	
	Needing Bodies	−4.0	Symbols
	Worshiping Bodies	−5.0	Eat
	Sacrifice	−6.0	Sex
	Hiding	−8.0	Mystery
	Being Objects	−10.0	Wait
	Being Nothing	−20.0	Unconscious
	Can't Hide	−30.0	
	Total Failure	−40.0	Unknowable

Know to Mystery Scale
[1978]

Tone Scale

40.0	Know
30.0	Not Know
22.0	Know About
20.0	Look
8.0	Plus Emotion
2.0	Minus Emotion
−1.5	Effort
−3.0	Think
−4.0	Symbols
−5.0	Eat
−6.0	Sex
−8.0	Mystery
−10.0	Wait
−20.0	Unconscious
−40.0	Unknowable

Communication Scale
[1951]

Speech: Talks	Tone Scale	Speech: Listens
	40.0	
	36.0 to 4.0	
Strong, able, swift and full exchange of beliefs and ideas.	4.0	Strong, able, swift and full exchange of beliefs and ideas.
Will talk of deep-seated beliefs and ideas.	3.5	Will accept deep-seated beliefs, ideas; consider them.
Tentative expression of limited number of personal ideas.	3.0	Receives ideas and beliefs if cautiously stated.
Casual pointless conversation.	2.5	Listens only to ordinary affairs.
Talks in threats. Invalidates other people.	2.0	Listens to threats. Openly mocks theta talk.
Talks of death, destruction, hate only.	1.5	Listens only to death and destruction. Wrecks theta lines.
Talks apparent theta, but intent vicious.	1.1	Listens little: mostly to cabal, gossip, lies.
Talks very little and only in apathetic tones.	0.5	Listens little: mostly to apathy or pity.
Does not talk.	0.1	Does not listen.
	0.0	
	–1.0	
	–3.0	

Communication Scale
[1951]

Tone Scale	Handling of Written or Spoken Communication When Acting as a Relay Point
40.0	
36.0 to 4.0	
4.0	Passes theta communication, contributes to it. Cuts entheta lines.[1]
3.5	Passes theta communication. Resents and hits back at entheta lines.
3.0	Passes communication. Conservative. Inclines toward moderate construction and creation.
2.5	Cancels any communication of higher or lower tone. Devaluates urgencies.
2.0	Deals in hostile or threatening communication. Lets only small amount of theta go through.
1.5	Perverts communication to entheta regardless of original content. Stops theta communication. Passes on entheta and perverts it.
1.1	Relays only malicious communication. Cuts comm lines. Won't relay.
0.5	Takes little heed of communication. Does not relay.
0.1	Does not relay. Unaware of communication.
0.0	MEST body, no communication. Theta not certainly contactable by existing technology.
–1.0	MEST body, no communication. Theta not certainly contactable by existing technology.
–3.0	Same as –1.0.

---

1. **entheta lines:** communication lines which are slanderous, choppy or destructive in an attempt to overwhelm or suppress a person or group. *Entheta* is short for enturbulated theta (thought or life).

Emotion Scale
[1951]

Tone Scale

40.0

36.0 to 4.0

4.0	Eagerness, exhilaration.
3.5	Strong interest.
3.0	Mild interest.
	Content.
2.5	Indifference. Boredom.
2.0	Expressed resentment.
1.5	Anger.
1.1	Unexpressed resentment. Fear.
0.5	Grief.
	Apathy.
0.1	Deepest apathy.
0.0	
−1.0	
−3.0	

Affinity Scale
[1951]

Tone Scale

40.0

36.0 to 4.0

4.0	Love, strong, outgoing.
3.5	Tentative advances, friendliness.
3.0	Tolerance without much outgoing action. Acceptance of advances offered.
2.5	Neglect of person or of people, withdrawal from them.
2.0	Antagonism.
1.5	Hate, violent and expressed.
1.1	Covert hostility.
1.0	Withdrawal from people. Acute shyness, propitiation.
0.5	Supplication, pleas for pity.
0.1	Complete withdrawal from person or people.
0.0	Cellular cohesion.
–1.0	Cellular cohesion.
–3.0	Normal physical laws of cohesion, adhesion.[1]

---

1. **adhesion:** *(physics)* the force that holds together the molecules of unlike substances whose surfaces are in contact: distinguished from cohesion. *See also* **cohesion** in the glossary.

Reality (Agreement) Scale
[1951]

Tone Scale

40.0

36.0 to 4.0

4.0   Search for different viewpoints in order to broaden own reality. Changes reality.

3.5   Ability to understand and evaluate reality of others and to change viewpoint. Agreeable.

3.0   Awareness of possible validity of different reality. Conservative agreement.

2.5   Refusal to match two realities. Indifference to conflict in reality. Too careless to agree or disagree.

2.0   Verbal doubt. Defense of own reality. Attempts to undermine others. Disagrees.

1.5   Destruction of opposing reality. "You're wrong." Disagrees with reality of others.

1.1   Doubt of own reality. Insecurity. Doubt of opposing reality.

0.5   Shame, anxiety, strong doubt of own reality. Easily has reality of others forced on him.

0.1   Complete withdrawal from conflicting reality. No reality.

0.0   Subjective reality none.

–1.0   Cellular reality.

–3.0   MEST reality.

Awareness Scale
(Scale of Reality)
[1955]

Aware of being aware

Awareness of an environment as sufficient communication

Knows of the existence of communication

Communication with the intent to communicate

Communication with significance with somebody else

Communication with significance

Communication with self with significance (worry)
(Even here, some slight awareness that he is thinking a thought and communicating with the thought he is thinking)

Unconsciousness (absolute unconsciousness is, however, unobtainable)

Reality Scale
[1957]

Tone Scale

40.0	Postulates
	Considerations
	Agreements
	Masses (Terminals) (Havingness Scale fits in here.)
0.0	Solid communication lines

Reality-Spotting by E-Meter
[1967]

Needle characteristics plotted on scale with numerical tone scale values, "old" Reality Scale and "new" Reality Scale.

TONE SCALE	REALITY SCALE (OLD—1957)	REALITY SCALE (NEW—1967)	NEEDLE CHARACTERISTICS
40 to 20	Postulates	Pan-determined Creation	Produces meter phenomena at will.
20 to 4	Consideration	Self-determined Creation	Free needle.
4 to 2	Agreements	Experience	Free needle, drop at will.
1.5	Solid terminals	Confront	Drop.
1.1	Terminals too solid Lines solid	Elsewhereness	Theta Bop.
1 to 0.5	No terminal Solid line	Invisibility	Stuck, sticky.
0.5 to 0.1	No terminal Less solid line	Blackness	
0.1	No real terminal No solid line Substitute terminal	Dub-in (no confront, not-isness)	Rising needle.
0.0	No terminal No line	Unconsciousness	Stuck. Also stage four needle. (All machine—no pc.)

Behavior and Physiology Scale
[1951]

Tone Scale

40.0	Ultimate capabilities unknown.
36.0 to 4.0	Capabilities only partly explored.
4.0	Excellent at projects, execution. Fast reaction time (relative to age).
3.5	Good at projects, execution, sports.
3.0	Capable of fair amount of action, sports.
2.5	Relatively inactive, but capable of action.
2.0	Capable of destructive and minor constructive action.
1.5	Capable of destructive action.
1.1	Capable of minor execution.
0.5	Capable of relatively uncontrolled action.
0.1	Alive as an organism.
0.0	Cells alive.
–1.0	Cells alive.
–3.0	Inorganic chemicals.

Medical Range
[1951]

Tone Scale

40.0

36.0 to 4.0

4.0	Near accident-proof. No psychosomatic ills. Nearly immune to bacteria.
3.5	Highly resistant to common infections. No colds.
3.0	Resistant to infection and disease. Few psychosomatic ills.
2.5	Occasionally ill. Susceptible to usual diseases.
2.0	Severe sporadic illnesses.
1.5	Depository illnesses (arthritis). (Range 1.0 to 2.0 interchangeable.)
1.1	Endocrine and neurological illnesses.
0.5	Chronic malfunction of organs. (Accident prone.)
0.1	Chronically ill. (Refusing sustenance.)
0.0	Dead.
–1.0	Dead.
–3.0	Dead.

DEI Scale to CDEI Scale
[1951–71]

The original scale,

4.0 Desire

1.5 Enforce

.5 Inhibit

was expanded in 1952 to

Curiosity

Desire

Enforce

Inhibit.

In 1959 I found another vital point on this scale which gave us a new case entrance point,

Curiosity

Desire

Enforce

Inhibit

Unknown

I suspected also that "Wait" fits between Unknown and Inhibit.

To make these agree in intention, they would become

Interest

Desire

Enforce

Inhibit

Unknow.

This scale also inverts, I find, similar to the dynamics and below sanity on any subject,

> Unknow
>
> Inhibit
>
> Enforce
>
> Desire
>
> Interest

These points, particularly on the inverted scale, going down, are lowered by failure. Each lower step is an explanation to justify having failed with the upper level.

One seeks to not know something and fails. One then seeks to inhibit it and fails. Therefore one seeks to enforce it and fails. Thus one explains by desiring it and fails. And not really being able to have it shows thereafter an obsessive[1] interest in it.

The above inversion is of course all reactive.

In 1971 the scale was expanded to

> K Know
>
> U Unknow
>
> C Curious
>
> D Desire
>
> E Enforce
>
> I Inhibit
>
> N No
>
> R Refused

---

1. **obsessive:** of or having to do with an idea, wish, etc., that fills one's thoughts and cannot be put out of the mind by the person.

Scale of Knowingness
[1971]

Know

Not-Know

Know About

Forget

Remember

Occlude

Responsibility, at Tone Levels
[1952]

Tone Scale

40.0	Full responsibility; responsibility manifests itself as will, can be so pervasive there is no randomity.
20.0	Responsibility manifests itself in terms of action where roughly half the environment or space has been selected for randomity and for which one is taking no responsibility; 50 percent of the total energy existing.
4.0	Disagreeing, by using the emotion of enthusiasm, with an existing state of affairs, directing energy toward the righting of that state of affairs. Responsibility is low at this level.
2.0	This is the level of the Tone Scale where fault is envisioned for the first time. Above this level there is sufficient breadth of understanding to see that interdependencies and randomities can exist without fault or blame. Blame; assigning blame for lack of responsibility rather than trying to enforce responsibility.
1.5	Blame is almost sole activity; takes no real responsibility himself, yet blames all on the environment and does so with violence.
1.1	Pretends to take responsibility in order to demonstrate that others are at fault, but has no real responsibility.
0.9	Willing to accept all blame in an effort to escape all punishment; doesn't think in terms of responsibility.
0.75	Individual blames himself and accepts the fault for what has occurred.
0.375	No question of either blame or responsibility; one has become MEST.

Responsibility Scale
[1962]

The deterioration of pan-determinism[1] over a game into "no responsibility" is as follows:

No Previous or Current Contact	=	No responsibility or liability.
Pan-determinism	=	Full responsibility for both sides of game.
Other-determinism	=	No responsibility for other side of game.
Self-determinism	=	Full responsibility for self, no responsibility for other side of game.
Valence (Circuit)	=	No responsibility for the game, for either side of the game or for a former self.

---

1. **pan-determinism:** the willingness to start, change and stop two or more forces, whether or not opposed, and this could be interpreted as two or more individuals, two or more groups, two or more planets, two or more life-species, two or more universes, two or more spirits, whether or not opposed. This means that one would not necessarily choose sides.

Scale of Motion
[1951]

Tone Scale

40.0

36.0 to 4.0

4.0	Rational use of all possible motions to fit the situation. Motion toward, swift approach.
3.5	Motion toward, slower approach.
3.0	Slow motion; consideration of effects of outside motion.
2.5	Watches motion. Slow motion away.
2.0	Changes motion and gets rid of it. Motion away, swift.
	Motion toward, slow attack.
1.5	Tries to hold everything still. Stops motion. Motion toward, violent attack.
1.1	Covertly tries to stop motion. Motion away, slow retreat.
0.9	Motion away, violent.
0.5	Moves with motion from outside. Slight motion, agitation in one place; suffer.
0.1	Motion goes through. "Endure."
0.0	Zero motion.

–1.0

–3.0

Cycle of Action Scale
[1952]

An assessment[1] of a case can be done by use of the following graph. We see here "create" with an arrow pointing straight downward and find there the words "If only this, insane on subject," and, under this, we list the dynamics.

Wherever along any of the dynamics the individual cannot conceive himself to be able to create, on that level he will be found aberrated to the degree that he does not believe himself able to create.

This might be thought to introduce an imponderable,[2] but such is not the case, for the individual is most aberrated on the first dynamic and, rightly or wrongly, conceives that he could not create himself. This goes to the extent, in *Homo sapiens*, of believing that one cannot create a body and, rightly or wrongly, one is then most aberrated on the subject of his body.

Potentially, because of the character of theta itself, an individual in an absolute and possibly unattainable state should be able to create a universe. Certainly it is true that every man is his own universe and possesses within himself all the capabilities of a universe.

To the extreme right of the graph we have the word "destroy" and an arrow pointing downwards toward insanity and, beneath this, the list of the dynamics.

That individual who can only destroy along any of these dynamics and cannot or will not create could be said to be

---

1. **assessment:** an inventory and evaluation of a preclear, his body and his case to establish processing level and procedure.

2. **an imponderable:** something which cannot be conclusively determined or explained.

aberrated on that dynamic. He is aberrated to the degree that he would destroy that dynamic.

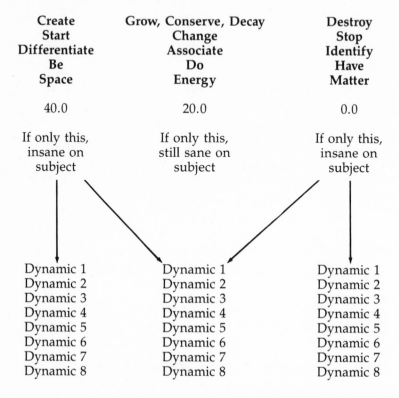

Create	Grow, Conserve, Decay	Destroy
Start	Change	Stop
Differentiate	Associate	Identify
Be	Do	Have
Space	Energy	Matter
40.0	20.0	0.0
If only this, insane on subject	If only this, still sane on subject	If only this, insane on subject

Dynamic 1	Dynamic 1	Dynamic 1
Dynamic 2	Dynamic 2	Dynamic 2
Dynamic 3	Dynamic 3	Dynamic 3
Dynamic 4	Dynamic 4	Dynamic 4
Dynamic 5	Dynamic 5	Dynamic 5
Dynamic 6	Dynamic 6	Dynamic 6
Dynamic 7	Dynamic 7	Dynamic 7
Dynamic 8	Dynamic 8	Dynamic 8

Looking again at the column of creation, one finds the individual aberrated anywhere along the dynamics in that column where the individual will only create and will not destroy.

In the destruction column one finds the individual aberrated on any dynamic in that column where he will not destroy.

In the middle ground of the graph we find that a balance of creation and destruction is sanity, and in the dynamics below it we find the individual sane wherever he will create and destroy.

Use of this graph and these principles will enable the auditor to assess hitherto hidden compulsions and obsessions on the part of the preclear.

The Tone Scale of Decisions
[1952]

Unaberrated conduct to a marked degree is

the making of decisions which can be put into effect

as opposed to

making decisions which cannot be put into effect

and down to

indecision

and lower to

irrational decision to force irrational decision into effect,

down to

indecision

and down to

the decision not to be.

Postulate Tone Scale
[1951]

Tone Scale

	I-they-I (To some degree, I am them because I don't have to worry about it. I take good care of them.)
27.0 to 40.0	I am.
10.0 or 11.0	I am and they need me.
3.5 to 4.0	I'm working with them.
2.5	I'm even with them and I don't like it.
2.0	I'll be despite them.
1.5	I'll be if I destroy them.
1.1	I would be if I could get around them.
0.5	I am not because they won't let me.
0.0	I am not.

The Chart of Attitudes
[1952]

Survives	Fully Responsible
Dead	No Responsibility
Everyone	Motion Source
Nobody	Stopped
Faith	Cause
Distrust	Full Effect
Win	Difference
Lose	Identification
Right	Owns All
Wrong	Owns Nothing
Always	Truth
Never	Hallucination
I Am	I Know
I Am Not	I Know Not
Start	Being
Stop	Had

On this chart, the upper line of each pair represents from 27.0 to 40.0. The lower line of each pair represents 0.0.

Each one of these is a gradient scale with many intermediate points.

The Dichotomies
[1952]

1. Survive
   Succumb

2. Affinity
   No Affinity

3. Communication
   No Communication

4. Agree
   Disagree

5. Start
   Stop

6. Be
   Be Not

7. Know
   Know Not

8. Cause
   Effect

9. Change
   No Change

10. Win
    Lose

11. I Am
    I Am Not

12. Faith
    Distrust

13. Imagine
    Truth

14. Believe
    Not Believe

15. Always
    Never

16. Future
    Past

17. Everyone
    Nobody

18. Owns All
    Owns Nothing

19. Responsible
    Not Responsible

20. Right
    Wrong

21. Stay
    Escape

22. Beauty
    Ugliness

23. Reason
    Emotion

24. Emotion
    Effort

25. Effort
    Apathy

26. Acceptance
    Rejection

27. Sane
    Insane

28. No-sympathy
    Sympathy

29. Sympathy
    Propitiation

Table of Related Experiences
[1952]

There is a table of relationships which the auditor must have. These are divided into three general columns. Any one of the columns may be addressed first, but all three columns must be addressed on any subject. The vertical levels of the columns can be considered to be terms which are synonymous.[1]

40.0	20.0	0.0
Start	Change	Stop
Space	Energy	Time
Beingness	Doingness	Havingness
Positive	Current	Negative
Creation	Alteration	Destruction
Conception	Living	Death
Differentiation	Association	Identification

ARC applies to each column or for any one of the above statements of experience.

All eight dynamics apply to each column and thus to any of the above statements of experience.

---

1. **synonymous:** equivalent or similar in meaning.

Games Conditions[1]
[1956]

In the following list we have the most processable games conditions and the most-to-be-avoided no-games conditions.

Each column of the list could be KNOWING or UNKNOWING— "knowing games condition" or "unknowing games condition," "knowing no-games condition" or "unknowing no-games condition."

Using both lists at a knowing games level, we have sanity. At an unknowing games level we have aberration, neurosis[2] or psychosis.[3]

Games Condition (Knowing or Unknowing)	No-Games Condition (Knowing or Unknowing)
Not-know	Know
Forget	Remember
Interest	
Disinterest	
Attention	No Attention
Self-determinism	Pan-determinism
Identity (runs as "Individuality")	Namelessness

(continued on next page)

---

1. **games conditions:** the factors which make a game, which is a contest of person against person or team against team. A game consists of freedoms, barriers and purposes, and there is a necessity in a game to have an opponent or an enemy. Also there is a necessity to have problems, and enough individuality to cope with a situation. To live life fully, then, one must have in addition to "something to do," a higher purpose, and this purpose, to be a purpose at all, must have counter-purposes or purposes which prevent it from occurring. This last is very important: If a person lacks problems, opponents and counter-purposes to his own, he will invent them. Here we have in essence the totality of aberration.

2. **neurosis:** a condition wherein a person is insane or disturbed on some subject (as opposed to psychosis, wherein a person is just insane in general).

3. **psychosis:** *see* **neurosis** above.

Games Condition *(cont.)* (Knowing or Unknowing)	No-Games Condition *(cont.)* (Knowing or Unknowing)
Problems	Solutions
Can't Have (games have some havingness)	Have
Alive	Neither Alive nor Dead
Opponents	Friends/Alone
Facsimiles	No Pictures or Universes
Continued Solidity	No Spaces or Solids
Continued Adherence[4] Loyalty, Disloyalty Betrayal, Help (these are all buttons that work)	No Friends or Enemies
Motion	No Motion
Emotion	Serenity
Continued Action	Motionless
Hot/Cold	No Temperature
Thinking	Knowing
Hate	
Some Love	
Continued Doubt of Result (expecting a revelation[5])	Win/Lose
No Effect on Self and Effect on Others	Effect on Self and No Effect on Others
Stop Communication	No ARC
Change Communication	No No-ARC
Into It	Out of It
Agitation	Calm
Noise	Silence
Some Silence	
Control (Start-Change-Stop Change the most important)	No Control
Responsibility	No Responsibility

---

4. **adherence:** the action of remaining faithful to or continuing to support.

5. **revelation:** a revealing; the making known of something that was secret or hidden.

Scale of Identification
[1952]

Tone Scale

40.0	Differentiate
20.0	
	Associate
0.0	Identify
—	Disassociate
—	
—	
—	
−8.0	

Pan-determinism Scale
[1955]

Pan-determinism:	A willingness to start, change and stop on any and all dynamics; the willingness to start, change and stop two or more forces, whether or not opposed. (This could be interpreted as two or more individuals, two or more groups, two or more planets, two or more life-species, two or more universes, two or more spirits, etc., whether or not opposed.) Would not necessarily fight, would not necessarily choose sides.
Fighting:	A willingness to fight things.
Must/Must not happen again:	Willingness to associate and repair somewhat, but no willingness to let certain things happen again.
Repair:	Willingness to associate and repair somewhat.
Association:	Unwillingness to repair anything; willingness to associate somewhat. Unwillingness to associate with anything.

Prehavingness Scale

[1961]

65. Faith
64. Cause
63a. Prevent Knowing
63. No Effect
62. Effect
61. Obsessive Can't Have
60a. Make Something of
60. Create
59. Think
58. Inverted Interest
    (Peculiar Interest)
57. Disperse
56. Inverted Communication
    (Intend to Not Communicate)
55. Inverted Control
54. Inverted Help (Betray)
53. Collect
52. Substitute (Failed Attack)
51. Withdraw
50. Duplicate
49. Enter
48. Inhibit
47. Disagree
46. Enforce
45. Agree
44. Desire
43. Know
42. Failed to Endure
41. Endure
40. No Motion
39. Failed to Abandon
38. Abandon

(continued on next page)

37. Failed Waste
36. Waste
35. Failed to Protect
34. Protect
33a. Make Nothing of
33. Failed Leave
32. Leave
31. Wait
30. Survive
29. Failed to Arrive
28. Arrive
27. Failed Importance
26. Importance
25. Propitiate
24. Attention
23. Separate
22. Failed Withhold
21. Withhold
20. Misemotional
19. Destroy
18. Motion
17. Failed Overt
16. Overts (Attack)
15. Dislike
14. Like
13. Compete
12. Failed Help
11. Help
10. Failed Control
9. Control
8. Emotional
7. Failed Communication
6. Communication
5. Failed Interest
4. Interest
3. Connect
2. Failed Havingness
1. Havingness

Havingness Scale
[1960]

Create

Responsible for
  (willing to control)

Contribute to

Confront

Have

Waste

Substitute

Waste Substitute

Had

Must be Confronted

Must be Contributed to

Created

Robotism Scale
[1972]

The individual with an evil purpose has to withhold himself because he may do destructive things.

When he fails to withhold himself, he commits overt acts on his fellows or other dynamics and occasionally loses control and does so.

This of course makes him quite inactive.

To overcome this, he refuses any responsibility for his own actions.

Any motion he makes must be on the responsibility of others.

He operates, then, only when given orders.

Thus, he must have orders to operate.

Therefore, one could term such a person a *robot*. And the malady could be called *robotism*.

There is a scale which shows the robot band:

Pan-determined

Self-determined

Robot band
- Other-determined
- Oblivious

Insane

Effect Scale
[1960]

From: Can cause or receive   40.0
         any effect

To: Must cause total effect,   0.0
         can receive none

To: Is total effect, is   −8.0
         hallucinatory cause

Effects (on Self, on Others) at Tone Levels

[1960]

Two Rules for Happy Living:

1. Be able to experience anything.

2. Cause only those things which others can experience easily.

The way a preclear receives an effect (effect tolerable on self) and the way he acts toward others, including the auditor (effect believed necessary on others) can be observed by an auditor and used to spot the preclear's tone level, either chronic or temporary, on any or all dynamics.

These are some examples of what might be observed at different tone levels.

Enthusiasm

Effect tolerable on self: Can receive large effects on self (the man who loses his fortune and bounces back). He is willing to receive other people's opinions, can accept large changes, he knows he has had a case change and is willing to change. He can accept defeats and will persist. Does not compulsively prevent effect on self.

Effect believed necessary on others: He has considerable ability to create effects on others but is not under compulsion to create effects, he is not compelled to affect other people's lives, he grants beingness, can tolerate differences in people.

Conservatism

Effect tolerable on self: Not very willing to receive effects that change the status quo.[1] Not willing to be questioned on some subjects, not willing to have other people's attention directed to him such as being pointed out in a crowd, wearing outstanding clothes, etc.

Effect believed necessary on others: Believes effects which preserve the status quo are necessary. Somewhat cautious about creating an effect, withholds those things he thinks might hurt your feelings, or that you might not approve of. Believes he should not create too much effect but should be "one of the crowd." Should respect the privacy of others.

Boredom

Effect tolerable on self: Will receive any effect which produces a pleasant randomity, wants to be entertained but otherwise doesn't like to be shifted. Can't be bothered with most ideas and puts off any action.

Effect believed necessary on others: Doesn't need to do anything about anything, no compulsion to do or not to do (no action either).

Antagonism

Effect tolerable on self: Can tolerate effect on self up to a point. May be critical[2] of changes, resent things happening to him. Doesn't want to be the effect of certain things, others' opinions, actions, etc., and hurls back these effects from self by being critical.

---

1. **status quo:** the existing state of affairs (at a particular time).
2. **critical:** tending to find fault.

Effect believed necessary on others: Feels he must make others the recipient of their own effects, compulsively must threaten others to protect self.

Anger

Effect tolerable on self: Can't receive an effect on self and is fighting to ensure this. Pc stuck in an anger incident may manifest this in his inability to receive changes, affinity, others' reality, communication, etc.

Effect believed necessary on others: Must destroy anything that tries to create effect on him.

Covert Hostility

Effect tolerable on self: Cannot tolerate much effect on self. Tries to slip out of being an effect by covert means. Gives the impression of taking an order, etc., while holding a destructive intent, and no intention to actually do it.

Effect believed necessary on others: Believes a large effect is necessary to handle others, is incapable of doing this in any other than a covert way. Must cause an effect but is unwilling to be known as the cause of bad effects. If accused of having created bad effects he will claim his intention was good. This pc will make excuses, will make all sorts of "conditions" in doing a process, will try to give an answer that will satisfy the auditor, without actually doing the command.

Fear

Effect tolerable on self: This person can take so little effect that he runs from the slightest thing, jumps at a door slam, etc. A pc in *fear* will manifest this by stiffness, leaning back in his chair, whistling during a session[3] (whistling in the dark),[4] he may turn pale, shake, cold sweat, avoid answering questions, squirm, laugh nervously, try to get out of session, etc.

Effect believed necessary on others: Believes the effect he would have to create to overcome those things which overwhelm him is huge—so huge that he would rather go elsewhere than confront it. May make a lot of logical excuses to get out of being an effect (going upscale to covert hostility).

Propitiation

Effect tolerable on self: Very little, does "favors" to protect himself against bad effects. Will try to appease the auditor to avoid continuing the process.

Effect believed necessary on others: Propitiative actions.

Grief

Effect tolerable on self: Tolerable effect would be the acquisition of tokens of a better time. Pc with grief "just under the surface" may not be able to tolerate direct questioning on his problem without getting a lump in his throat or being brought to tears. Someone else's grief might be enough effect to cause him to cry. A rough word might not be tolerable.

Effect believed necessary on others: Believes that a large effect would have to be created to overcome his overwhelming opposition, but the idea of creating an effect on others produces the idea of loss and though he must create vast effects, he is very

---

3. **session:** a precise period of time during which an auditor audits a preclear.

4. **whistling in the dark:** trying to be courageous or hopeful in a fearful or trying situation.

close to the idea that he cannot create *any* effect, thus the only thing he can do about it is cry.

Apathy

Effect tolerable on self: Can accept even less effect here. This is the "no-effect case." Believes that everything is useless anyway, therefore nothing could make any difference to him. He will tell you that nothing is workable (apathetically).

Effect believed necessary on others: Believes that an infinite amount of effect must be created to get anything done. (That's why he is in apathy.)

Subapathy

A state of disinterest, no affinity, no reality, no communication. There will be social machinery, valences, circuits, etc., but the preclear himself will not be *there.*

As one proceeds down the subzero scale there is an increasing amount of hallucinatory cause, wherein the thetan considers that he is actually being more cause. This is the exact reverse of the reality of the situation. He is becoming more and more effect. Thus the mystic who is "causing" things far away, etc.

In subapathy a person can tolerate considerable effects, *apparently.* This can fool you. The effects are not real and he does not experience them. While he believes all his effects must be created for him, he is unwilling to receive any.

As a person descends on the scale and becomes more and more in the state of Must Create Effects–Must Receive None, his ability to do either dwindles out.

Regret, on the subzero scale, could be expressed as "trying to undo effects," thus being less effect.

Blame, "Effects done are wrong."

Shame, "Effects one creates are unworthy, shouldn't have done it."

Ranges of Effect

Effect tolerable on self:

40.0   Infinite, any effect tolerable on self.

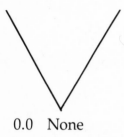

0.0   None

Effect believed necessary on others (i.e., to have reality on having created an effect):

40.0   None compulsive. Knows he can create effects.

0.0   Has to create total effect to have reality on creating any effects.

Subzero

Effect tolerable on self:

0.0   No effect tolerable on self

−8.0   No effect on self is real (i.e., perceived) but all causes do effect self. (Mockery of 40.0)

Effect believed necessary on others:

0.0   Must cause total effect (although *can* cause little or no effect).

−8.0   Can actually cause nothing but "causes everything" (unreality), e.g., "I caused the death of Pope Pius," when speaker was six thousand miles away.

Scale of Confront
[1959]

Beingness

Experience, or Participate

Ability to confront

Elsewhereness
(solution is "be elsewhere")

Invisibility ("it's just not there")

Blackness

Dub-in[1] (puts something else there)

---

1. **dub-in:** any unknowingly created mental picture that appears to have been a record of the physical universe but is, in fact, only an altered copy of the time track. It is a phrase out of the motion-picture industry of putting a sound track on top of something that isn't there.

The State of Case Scale
[1963]

Charge, the stored quantities of energy in the time track,[1] is the sole thing that is being relieved or removed by the auditor from the time track.

When this charge is present in hugh amounts, the time track overwhelms the pc and the pc is thrust below observation of the actual track. This is the State of Case Scale. (All levels given are major levels. Minor levels exist between them.)

Level (1)	NO TRACK	—	No charge.
Level (2)	FULL VISIBLE TIME TRACK	—	Some charge.
Level (3)	SPORADIC VISIBILITY OF TRACK	—	Some heavily charged areas.
Level (4)	INVISIBLE TRACK (Black or Invisible Field)[2]	—	Very heavily charged areas exist.
Level (5)	DUB–IN	—	Some areas of track so heavily charged pc is below unconsciousness in them.
Level (6)	DUB–IN OF DUB–IN	—	Many areas of track so heavily charged, the dub-in is submerged.
Level (7)	ONLY AWARE OF OWN EVALUATIONS	—	Track too heavily charged to be viewed at all.
Level (8)	UNAWARE	—	Pc dull, often in a coma.[3]

---

1. **time track:** the consecutive record of mental image pictures which accumulates through a person's life or lives. It is very exactly dated.

2. **black or invisible field:** some part of a mental image picture where the preclear is looking at blackness or invisibility. It is part of some lock, secondary or engram that is black or invisible.

3. **coma:** a state of deep and prolonged unconsciousness caused by injury or disease.

On this new scale the very good, easy-to-run cases are at Level (3). Skilled engram running can handle down to Level (4). Engram running is useless from Level (4) down. Level (4) is questionable.

Level (1) is of course an OT.[4] Level (2) is the clearest Clear[5] anybody ever heard of. Level (3) can run engrams. Level (4) can run early track engrams if the running is skilled. Level (4) includes the Black V case. Level (5) has to be run on general ARC processes. Level (6) has to be run carefully on special ARC processes with lots of havingness. Level (7) responds to the CCHs. Level (8) responds only to Reach and Withdraw CCHs.

Pre-Dianetic and pre-Scientology mental studies were observations from Level (7) which considered Levels (5) and (6) and (8) the only states of case and oddly enough overlooked Level (7) entirely; all states of case were considered either neurotic or insane, with sanity either slightly glimpsed or decried.[6]

In actuality, on some portion of every time track in every case you will find each of the levels except (1) momentarily expressed. The above scale is devoted to chronic case level and

---

4. **OT:** Operating Thetan. It is a state of beingness. It is a being "at cause over matter, energy, space, time, form and life." *Operating* comes from "able to operate without dependency on things," and *Thetan* is the Greek letter theta (θ), which the Greeks used to represent *thought* or perhaps *spirit*, to which an *n* is added to make a noun in the modern style used to create words in engineering. It is also θ^n or "theta to the nth degree," meaning unlimited or vast.

5. **Clear:** the name of a state achieved through auditing, or an individual who has achieved this state. A Clear is a being who no longer has his own reactive mind. A Clear is an unaberrated person and is rational in that he forms the best possible solutions he can on the data he has and from his viewpoint. The Clear has no engrams which can be restimulated to throw out the correctness of computation by entering hidden and false data.

6. **decried:** spoken out against strongly and openly; denounced.

is useful in programing a case. But any case for brief moments or longer will hit these levels in being processed. This is the temporary case level found only in sessions on chronically higher-level cases when they go through a tough bit.

Time Sense, Deterioration Of
[1963]

As in earlier writings, time is actual but is also an apparency. (See *Dianetics 55!* or other similar material.) Time is measured by motion. Motion is matter with energy in space. Thus a person can conceive of time as only matter and energy in space, such as a clock or a planetary rotation. Time is actual. But the person has become so dependent on matter moving in space to tell time that his time sense has become dependent on matter, energy and space.

Time sense deteriorates to the degree that one has depended upon matter, energy and space to tell time.

The dwindling spiral[1] was as follows:

State A	—	Time sense.
State B	—	Time sense dependent upon matter, energy and space.
State C	—	ARC breaks with matter, energy, space and other beings.
State D	—	Deteriorated time sense.

Identification (A = A = A) is most easily present when time sense is awry;[2] therefore, the degree a person identifies different things establishes the degree of aberration.

---

1. **dwindling spiral:** a phenomenon of the ARC triangle whereby when one breaks some affinity, a little bit of the reality goes down, and then communication goes down, which makes it impossible to get affinity as high as before; so a little bit more gets knocked off affinity, and then reality goes down, and then communication. This is the dwindling spiral in progress, until it hits the bottom—death—which is no affinity, no communication and no reality.

2. **awry:** wrong; amiss.

Points of Case Address

1951:

       Thought

       Effort

       Emotion

1952: This scale was modified to:

       Aesthetics

       Reason

       Emotion

       Effort

Scale of Relative Success in Estimating Efforts (Scale of Potential Survival)

[1952]

Tone Scale

4.0	Happiness	Few computations conflicting	Uses effort well
3.0	Conservatism	Many known conflicts	Uses effort cautiously
2.5	Boredom	Conflicts known but opposed	Uses effort poorly
2.0	Antagonism	Conflicts considered dangerous	Strikes back
1.5	Anger	Unknown conflicts balanced	Holds and destroys
1.1	Covert hostility	Many unknowns	Uses effort covertly
1.0	Fear	Sharply fixed on unknown; attention unfixed	Uses effort to withdraw
.75	Grief	Holds unknown pains	Has given up
.5	Apathy	Doesn't know or care	Effort uses him

Scale of Politics
[1969]

Here is a scale taken from "Excalibur" from memory. "Excalibur" was an unpublished book written in the very late 1930s. Only fragments of it remain.

By placing it against the Tone Scale developed at the end of 1950, certain current political philosophies are better estimated. By then looking up these tone characteristics in *Science of Survival* much can be learned and the ideologies are thus made easier to predict or handle.

Tone Scale

3.0	Republic
2.5	Democracy
2.0	Social Democracy
1.5	Fascism
1.1	Communism
0.0	Anarchism

The cycle of a nation goes on a descending spiral down this scale.

Those two tones apart are not likely to fight. Those a tone apart fight seldom. Those a half tone apart are in continual conflict.

As this was worked out before World War II, it is quite remarkable to see how true it has held. And how each one has taken something from its neighbors.

I will not go into what lies above democracy except that man is trying with his ideologies to solve mainly the problem of succession. History has seen other government forms work far more ideally than those named but in none of these could one guarantee succession of the beneficial rule. Thus adherents to all forms of ideology can be made to agree that "benign monarchy" is an excellent form of government. But they discard it because a truly good benign monarch is not necessarily succeeded by one in the next reign.

Few governments exist in pure form. (Note there are no major governments at this writing above Social Democracy.)

9

Perceptics and Awareness Characteristics

List of Perceptics
[1978]

This was researched and dates of 1951. It is a list of the 57 human perceptions.

1. Time
2. Sight
3. Taste
4. Color
5. Depth
6. Solidity (Barriers)
7. Relative Sizes (External)
8. Sound
9. Pitch
10. Tone
11. Volume
12. Rhythm
13. Smell (The sense of smell has four subdivisions which are categories of the type of odor.)
14. Touch
    a. Pressure
    b. Friction
    c. Heat or Cold
    d. Oiliness
15. Personal Emotion
16. Endocrine States
17. Awareness of Awareness
18. Personal Size
19. Organic Sensation (Including Hunger)

(continued on next page)

20. Heartbeat
21. Blood Circulation
22. Cellular and Bacterial Position
23. Gravitic[1] (Self and Other Weights)
24. Motion of Self
25. Motion (Exterior)
26. Body Position
27. Joint Position
28. Internal Temperature
29. External Temperature
30. Balance
31. Muscular Tension
32. Saline Content[2] of Self (Body)
33. Fields/Magnetic
34. Time Track Motion
35. Physical Energy
        (Personal Weariness, etc.)
36. Self-determinism
        (Relative on each Dynamic)
37. Moisture (Self)
38. Sound Direction
39. Emotional State of Other Organs
40. Personal Position on the Tone Scale
41. Affinity (Self and Others)
42. Communication (Self and Others)
43. Reality (Self and Others)
44. Emotional State of Groups
45. Compass Direction
46. Level of Consciousness

(continued on next page)

---

1. **gravitic:** of or having to do with weight or heaviness.
2. **saline content:** a sense of the salt content (of the body).

47. Pain
48. Perception of Conclusions
     (Past and Present)
49. Perception of Computation
     (Past and Present)
50. Perception of Imagination
     (Past and Present)
51. Perception of Having Perceived
     (Past and Present)
52. Awareness of Not Knowing
53. Awareness of Importance,
     Unimportance
54. Awareness of Others
55. Awareness of Location and Placement
     a. Masses
     b. Spaces
     c. Location Itself
56. Perception of Appetite
57. Kinesthesia[3]

---

3. **kinesthesia:** the sensation of position, movement, tension, etc., of parts of the body.

Awareness Characteristics
[1965]

21. Source
20. Existence
19. Conditions
18. Realization
17. Clearing
16. Purposes
15. Ability
14. Correction
13. Result
12. Production
11. Activity
10. Prediction
9. Body
8. Adjustment
7. Energy
6. Enlightenment
5. Understandings
4. Orientation
3. Perception
2. Communication
1. Recognition

Negative States
-1. Help
-2. Hope
-3. Demand for Improvement
-4. Need of Change
-5. Fear of Worsening
-6. Effect

(continued on next page)

-7. Ruin
-8. Despair
-9. Suffering
-10. Numbness
-11. Introversion
-12. Disaster
-13. Inactuality
-14. Delusion
-15. Hysteria
-16. Shock
-17. Catatonia
-18. Oblivion
-19. Detachment
-20. Duality
-21. Secrecy
-22. Hallucination
-23. Sadism
-24. Masochism
-25. Elation
-26. Glee
-27. Fixidity[1]
-28. Erosion
-29. Dispersal
-30. Disassociation
-31. Criminality
-32. Uncausing
-33. Disconnection
-34. Unexistence

---

1. **fixidity:** rigid or immobile; stationary or unchanging in relative position; fixed.

10

Abilities Gained

From Clear to Eternity
Ron's Journal 35

[1982]

As I continue to research, I never cease to be amazed at the amount of gain potentially available to an individual.

There are six rough divisions of case gain:[1]

1. From raw public to a realization Scientology works and should be continued.

2. The realization that, through his auditing, one will not get any worse—an arrested decline.

3. The whole band of gains we call the lower Grades.[2] The very least of these gains (and there are many by pc testimony) is stated to exceed by far any advance in personal gain ever before achieved in any former practice known. (A simple flying of ruds[3] can get more gain than ten years of psychoanalysis!)

---

1. **case gain:** the improvements and resurgences a person experiences from auditing; any case betterment according to the pc.

2. **Grades:** each Grade is a series of processes which are run on a preclear with the purpose of bringing him to a particular state of Release. The Grades encompass Expanded ARC Straightwire, Expanded Lower Grades 0–IV, Grade V, Grade VA and Grade VI. *See also* **Expanded Lower Grades** in the glossary.

3. **flying of ruds:** the addressing (taking up) and handling of rudiments (those steps or actions used to get the pc in shape to be audited) by taking his attention off any current upsets or worries or other distractions that might make it difficult for him to be audited.

4. The band that achieves, in a final burst of glory and freedom, the state of Clear.

5. The pre-OT levels,[4] leading to personal spiritual freedom. These carry up through all NOTs, Audited and Solo.[5] What is amazing here is that each one of these levels, according to rave reports, has, each one, its own spectacular level of gain.

6. The actual OT levels beginning now with New OT VIII and going on up.

According to the spiritual research records and pre-OT[6] and OT reports, the *amount* of gain available to one person is never really conceived, in an aberrated state, to potentially exist above him.

It is a never-ending source of wonder to people, going truly on this route, that there could be such *quantity* of gain available to one being.

Thus in an aberrated state, the person is not likely to turn his eyes up very high and still keep a reality on it.

---

4. **pre-OT levels:** the advanced auditing levels after Clear and preparatory to the actual OT levels which begin at New OT VIII. The pre-OT levels are New OT I through New OT VII. *See also* **pre-OT** in the glossary.

5. **NOTs, Audited and Solo:** *NOTs* is short for *New Era Dianetics for OTs*, a pre-OT level consisting of a series of confidential rundowns delivered by a specially trained OT auditor. Some of the mysteries of life have been exposed to full view for the first time ever in NOTs. *Solo NOTs* is audited by the pre-OT solo (meaning audited on oneself). The end phenomena of Solo NOTs is *Cause Over Life*.

6. **pre-OT:** a thetan beyond the state of Clear who, through the pre-OT levels, is advancing to the full state of Operating Thetan (OT). *See also* **pre-OT levels** in the glossary.

In the age of speed, people may conceive it all should happen in a minute. Or maybe a minute and a half. Or as the result of a needle jab which will make them free forever.

Alas, this universe isn't built that way.

This universe is based on *quantity.* There's an awful lot of it.

The number of electrons in an atom, the number of atoms in a molecule, the number of molecules in a drop of water is awesome arithmetic.

The number of planets in systems, the number of suns in a galaxy, the number of galaxies add up to mind-boggling figures.

Time, on this very short-lifed and hectic planet, is hardly conceived of at all. Just recently geologists concluded that man might have been here for a million years. HAH! Little do they know!

The age of this and other universes is very, very long. It is not eternity but almost.

So, without getting into questions as to how long you've been around (the brain-theory boys might object since they are *terrified* of spirits), let's ask this question:

If a being had half an eternity to louse himself up, how loused up could he get?

Right. Go to the head of the class. Plenty!

And you now can get an inkling of how much spiritual gain might be available. And this could explain why, at each one of the six levels, there are so many new gains according to testimonies collected.

All right. Got that? Good.

We now come to the next question, since one and all are being very bright this morning:

If it took a being half an eternity to louse himself up, how long would it take to unlouse him?

Now before your mouth turns down at both sides and before you collapse into apathy considering it, let's look at the next miracle of Dianetics and Scientology.

It doesn't take half an eternity. It doesn't take millennia— though this could be reasonably expected. It doesn't take centuries. It only takes years.

That's right. Years.

The above six rough divisions of gains are sort of an expanding scale.

The first one could take, with an intro or assist,[7] maybe half an hour plus a few evenings reading books.

The next level (consisting of formal auditing and Purif[8]) possibly could take a week or two.

---

7. **assist:** a simple, easily done process that can be applied to anyone to help them recover more rapidly from accidents, mild illness or upsets; any process which assists the individual to heal himself or be healed by another agency by removing his reasons for precipitating (bringing on) and prolonging his condition and lessening his predisposition (inclination or tendency) to further injure himself or remain in an intolerable condition.

8. **Purif:** short for Purification Rundown. *See* **Purification Rundown** in the glossary.

The third level, consisting of the lower Grades and more books could, due to scheduling of time and all that, consume a month.

The fourth level, depending on the case, might take a bit longer. But it can result in *Clear*.

The fifth band now begins to really lengthen. To become a Solo Auditor and go up through the levels to OT III could take months. And through OT III can stretch out considerably. And then Audited NOTs and Solo NOTs really adds time on. The gains at each point of progress can make, according to reports of pcs, progress at the lower end look like inches. Yet the lowest of these bands is above any progress man had made before.

Now when we get to band six, get ready for a long haul. It won't happen in a minute.

So what we're looking at here is time proportional to reported gain.

Once one has gone Clear and gets to Solo, one has to plan one's time to each day put his auditing time in and just keep at it.

Some balk when they have gone a week. Life looks too interesting. Or they bog and are "too busy" to get a repair to get them going again. They are, after all, moving at a much faster pace personally—their interests may have multiplied.

But if they will just keep at it and make the arrangements necessary to be able to do it, according to the rave reports, it is very worthwhile.

So what is one really looking at? The higher the level, the longer the time—because one is handling a higher band of potential gain.

And what is one rising to, after all?

One is rising to eternity.

You think time is behind you?

Have another thought. Look *ahead.*

There's eternity!

And you'll be in it.

You'll be in it in a good state or a bad one. Really, I'm sorry to have to tell you, there's no choice. One may be able to step off the planet. One isn't going to step off life.

In this time and in this place, for possibly just a little while, we have this chance. To go free and to make it. Planets and cultures are frail things. They do not endure.

I cannot promise you that you will make it. I can only provide the knowledge and give you your chance.

The rest is up to you.

I strongly advise you work hard at it—don't waste this brief breath in eternity.

For that is your future—ETERNITY.

It will be good for you or bad.

And for you, my dearest friend, I've done what I could to make it good for you.

Love, Ron

Chart of Abilities Gained
[1985]

LEVEL	ABILITY GAINED
GROUP PROCESSES [1]	Awareness that change is available.
LIFE REPAIR [2]	Awareness of truth and the way to personal freedom.
PURIFICATION RUNDOWN [3]	Freedom from the restimulative effects of drug residuals and other toxins. [4]
OBJECTIVES [5]	Oriented in the present time of the physical universe.
SCIENTOLOGY DRUG RUNDOWN [6]	Released from harmful effects of drugs, medicine or alcohol.

1. **group processes:** auditing techniques administered to groups of children or adults by a group auditor.

2. **Life Repair:** a series of auditing actions run on a preclear who is starting out in auditing for the first time. Life Repair would address such things as rough spots in life, periods which the preclear may feel bad about, areas of overwhelm, etc.

3. **Purification Rundown:** a special rundown (series of specific actions done on a case) designed to purify and clean out of one's system the restimulative drug or chemical residues which could act to prevent case gain from Dianetics or Scientology processing.

4. **toxins:** any of various poisonous compounds produced by some microorganisms and causing certain diseases.

5. **Objectives:** Objective Processes. *Objective* refers to outward things, not the thoughts or feelings of the individual. Objective Processes deal with the real and observable. They call for the preclear to spot or find something exterior to himself in order to carry out the auditing command. Objectives locate the person in his environment, establish direct communication with the auditor, and they bring a person to present time, a very important factor in mental and spiritual sanity and ability.

6. **Scientology Drug Rundown:** a rundown (series of auditing actions) which uses Scientology auditing techniques to handle the harmful effects of drugs, medicine and alcohol on a case. This rundown extroverts a person, brings him into present time, and allows him to experience the relief and expansion available to one who has been freed from the influence of drugs.

LEVEL	ABILITY GAINED
EXPANDED ARC STRAIGHTWIRE	Knows he/she won't get worse.

EXPANDED GRADE 0 COMMUNICATIONS RELEASE[7]

FLOW[8] 1:   Willing for others to communicate to him on any subject. No longer resisting communication from others on unpleasant or unwanted subjects.

FLOW 2:   Ability to communicate freely with anyone on any subject. Free from or no longer bothered by communication difficulties. No longer withdrawn or reticent.[9] Likes to outflow.

FLOW 3:   Willing for others to communicate freely to others about anything.

FLOW 0:   Willingness to permit oneself to communicate freely about anything.

---

7. **Release:** the term for what occurs when a person separates from his reactive mind or some part of it. The degree and relative permanence of being pulled out of the reactive mind determines the state of Release. There are a number of states or stages of Release and these are called Grades. *See also* **Grades; Expanded Lower Grades** in the glossary.

8. **flow:** the four flows referred to in the Chart of Abilities Gained are: Flow 1, something happening to self; Flow 2, doing something to another; Flow 3, others doing things to others; Flow 0, self doing something to self.

9. **reticent:** habitually silent or uncommunicative; reserved.

LEVEL   ABILITY GAINED

EXPANDED GRADE I
PROBLEMS RELEASE

FLOW 1:   No longer worried about problems others have been to self. Able to recognize the source of problems and make them vanish. Has no problems.

FLOW 2:   No longer worried about problems he has been to others. Feels free about any problems others may have with him and can recognize source of them.

FLOW 3:   Free from worry about others' problems with or about others, and can recognize source of them.

FLOW 0:   Free from worry about problems with self and can recognize the source of them.

EXPANDED GRADE II
RELIEF RELEASE

FLOW 1:   Freedom from things others have done to one in the past. Willing for others to be cause over him.

FLOW 2:   Relief from the hostilities and sufferings of life. Ability to be at cause without fear of hurting others.

FLOW 3:   Willing to have others be cause over others without feeling the need to intervene for fear of their doing harm.

FLOW 0:   Relief from hostilities and sufferings imposed by self upon self.

LEVEL   ABILITY GAINED

EXPANDED GRADE III
FREEDOM RELEASE

FLOW 1:   Freedom from upsets of the past.
          Ability to face the future. Ability to
          experience sudden change without
          becoming upset.

FLOW 2:   Can grant others the beingness to be
          the way they are and choose their
          own reality. No longer feels need to
          change people to make them more
          acceptable to self. Able to cause
          changes in another's life without ill
          effects.[10]

FLOW 3:   Freedom from the need to prevent or
          become involved in the change and
          interchange occurring amongst
          others.

FLOW 0:   Freedom from upsets of the past one
          has imposed upon oneself and ability
          to cause changes in one's own life
          without ill effects.

---

10. **ill effects:** harmful, bad or unfavorable consequences, developments or results.

LEVEL	ABILITY GAINED

EXPANDED GRADE IV
ABILITY RELEASE

FLOW 1: Free from and able to tolerate others' fixed ideas, justifications and make-guilty of self. Free of need to respond in a like manner.

FLOW 2: Moving out of fixed conditions into ability to do new things. Ability to face life without need to justify own actions or defend self from others. Loss of make-guilty mechanisms and demand for sympathy. Can be right or wrong.

FLOW 3: Can tolerate fixed conditions of others in regard to others. Freedom from involvement in others' efforts to justify, make guilty, dominate or be defensive about their actions against others.

FLOW 0: Ability to face life without need to make self wrong. Loss of make-self-guilty[11] mechanisms and self-invalidation.

---

11. **make-guilty:** the action of a person excusing or making another or others wrong or guilty. It is a mechanism used to dominate or escape domination and enhance one person's survival and injure that of others.

LEVEL	ABILITY GAINED
NEW ERA DIANETICS [12] *DRUG RUNDOWN*	Freedom from harmful effects of drugs, alcohol and medicine and free from the need to take them.
NEW ERA DIANETICS CASE COMPLETION	A well and happy preclear.

CLEAR

A being who no longer has his own reactive mind.

Alternate Clear Route, for those who did not go Clear on NED:

LEVEL	ABILITY GAINED
GRADE V POWER RELEASE	Ability to handle power.
GRADE VA POWER PLUS RELEASE	Stabilizes ability to handle power.
GRADE VI WHOLE TRACK [13] *RELEASE*	Return of powers to act on own determinism. Freedom from dramatization.
CLEARING COURSE	A being who no longer has his own reactive mind.

LEVEL	ABILITY GAINED
SUNSHINE RUNDOWN [14]	(As given in the materials of the Sunshine Rundown.)

12. **New Era Dianetics:** a summary and refinement of Dianetics based upon thirty years of experience in the application of the subject. New Era Dianetics was released in 1978 and New Era Dianetics auditing and training are today available in all Scientology organizations.

13. **whole track:** the moment-to-moment record of a person's existence in this universe in picture and impression form.

14. **Sunshine Rundown:** a special auditing step done by Clears after they attest to having attained the state of Clear.

The Pre-OT Levels

LEVEL	ABILITY GAINED
NEW OT I	(As given in the materials of New OT I.)
OT II	(As given in the materials of OT II.)
OT III	(As given in the materials of OT III.)
NEW OT IV *OT DRUG RUNDOWN*	(As given in the materials of New OT IV.)
NEW OT V *AUDITED NOTs*[15]	(As given in the materials of New OT V.)
NEW OT VI *HUBBARD SOLO NOTs* *AUDITING COURSE*[16]	(As given in the materials of New OT VI.)
NEW OT VII *SOLO NOTs*	(As given in the materials of New OT VII.)

---

15. **NOTs:** New Era Dianetics for OTs.

16. **Hubbard Solo NOTs Auditing Course:** the course which covers the materials necessary to be able to audit Solo NOTs; New OT VI. *See also* **Solo NOTs** in the glossary.

The OT Levels

LEVEL	ABILITY GAINED
NEW OT VIII *TRUTH REVEALED*	(As given in the materials of New OT VIII.)
NEW OT IX *ORDERS OF MAGNITUDE*	(As given in the materials of New OT IX.)
NEW OT X *CHARACTER*	(As given in the materials of New OT X.)
NEW OT XI *OPERATING*	(As given in the materials of New OT XI.)
NEW OT XII *FUTURE*	(As given in the materials of New OT XII.)
NEW OT XIII	(As given in the materials of New OT XIII.)
NEW OT XIV	(As given in the materials of New OT XIV.)
NEW OT XV	(As given in the materials of New OT XV.)

11

Codes and Principles of Conduct

The Code of a Scientologist

[1969]

As a Scientologist, I pledge myself to the Code of Scientology for the good of all.

1. To keep Scientologists, the public and the press accurately informed concerning Scientology, the world of mental health and society.

2. To use the best I know of Scientology to the best of my ability to help my family, friends, groups and the world.

3. To refuse to accept for processing and to refuse to accept money from any preclear or group I feel I cannot honestly help.

4. To decry and do all I can to abolish any and all abuses against life and mankind.

5. To expose and help abolish any and all physically damaging practices in the field of mental health.

6. To help clean up and keep clean the field of mental health.

7. To bring about an atmosphere of safety and security in the field of mental health by eradicating[1] its abuses and brutality.

---

1. **eradicating:** getting rid of; wiping out; destroying.

8. To support true humanitarian endeavors in the fields of human rights.

9. To embrace the policy of equal justice for all.

10. To work for freedom of speech in the world.

11. To actively decry the suppression of knowledge, wisdom, philosophy or data which would help mankind.

12. To support the freedom of religion.

13. To help Scientology orgs[2] and groups ally themselves with public groups.

14. To teach Scientology at a level it can be understood and used by the recipients.

15. To stress the freedom to use Scientology as a philosophy in all its applications and variations in the humanities.[3]

16. To insist upon standard and unvaried Scientology as an applied activity in ethics, processing and administration in Scientology organizations.

17. To take my share of responsibility for the impact of Scientology upon the world.

18. To increase the numbers and strength of Scientology over the world.

19. To set an example of the effectiveness and wisdom of Scientology.

20. To make this world a saner, better place.

---

2. **orgs:** *(Scientology slang)* organizations that deliver Dianetics and Scientology training and processing.

3. **humanities:** the branches of learning concerned with human thought and relations, as distinguished from the sciences; especially literature, philosophy, history, etc.

The Auditor's Code

[1980]

I hereby promise as an auditor to follow the Auditor's Code.

1. I promise not to evaluate[1] for the preclear or tell him what he should think about his case in session.

2. I promise not to invalidate the preclear's case or gains in or out of session.

3. I promise to administer only standard tech to a preclear in the standard way.

4. I promise to keep all auditing appointments once made.

5. I promise not to process a preclear who has not had sufficient rest and who is physically tired.

6. I promise not to process a preclear who is improperly fed or hungry.

7. I promise not to permit a frequent change of auditors.

---

1. **evaluate:** to impose data or knowledge upon another. An example would be to tell another why he is the way he is instead of permitting or guiding him to discover it for himself.

8. I promise not to sympathize with a preclear but to be effective.

9. I promise not to let the preclear end session on his own determinism but to finish off those cycles I have begun.

10. I promise never to walk off from a preclear in session.

11. I promise never to get angry with a preclear in session.

12. I promise to run every major case action to a floating needle.[2]

13. I promise never to run any one action beyond its floating needle.

14. I promise to grant beingness to the preclear in session.

15. I promise not to mix the processes of Scientology with other practices except when the preclear is physically ill and only medical means will serve.

16. I promise to maintain communication with the preclear and not to cut his comm[3] or permit him to overrun[4] in session.

17. I promise not to enter comments, expressions or enturbulence[5] into a session that distract a preclear from his case.

18. I promise to continue to give the preclear the process or auditing command when needed in the session.

19. I promise not to let a preclear run a wrongly understood command.

---

2. **floating needle:** the same as a free needle. *See* **free needle** in the glossary.

3. **cut his comm:** cut (stopped, halted) his communication.

4. **overrun:** continue a process or a series of processes past the optimum point.

5. **enturbulence:** turbulence; agitation; disturbance.

20. I promise not to explain, justify or make excuses in session for any auditor mistakes whether real or imagined.

21. I promise to estimate the current case state of a preclear only by standard case supervision[6] data and not to diverge[7] because of some imagined difference in the case.

22. I promise never to use the secrets of a preclear divulged[8] in session for punishment or personal gain.

23. I promise to never falsify worksheets of sessions.

24. I promise to see that any fee received for processing is refunded, following the policies of the Claims Verification Board,[9] if the preclear is dissatisfied and demands it within three months after the processing, the only condition being that he may not again be processed or trained.

25. I promise not to advocate[10] Dianetics or Scientology only to cure illness or only to treat the insane, knowing well they were intended for spiritual gain.

26. I promise to cooperate fully with the authorized organizations of Dianetics and Scientology in safeguarding the ethical use and practice of those subjects.

---

6. **case supervision:** referring to the actions of the Case Supervisor. The C/S is the auditor's "handler." He tells the auditor what to do, keeps him corrected, keeps the lines straight and keeps the auditor calm and willing and winning. The C/S directs what auditing actions are done for each individual preclear under his care. All case supervision is for the benefit of the preclear. *See also* **case(s)** in the glossary.

7. **diverge:** to depart from a given viewpoint, practice, etc.; differ.

8. **divulged:** made known; disclosed; revealed.

9. **Claims Verification Board:** an official group within the Church of Scientology which facilitates refund requests.

10. **advocate:** to speak or write in support of; be in favor of.

27. I promise to refuse to permit any being to be physically injured, violently damaged, operated on or killed in the name of "mental treatment."

28. I promise not to permit sexual liberties or violations of patients.

29. I promise to refuse to admit to the ranks of practitioners any being who is insane.

The Supervisor's Code

[1967]

1. The Supervisor must never neglect an opportunity to direct a student to the actual source of Scientology data.

2. The Supervisor should invalidate a student's mistakes ruthlessly and use good ARC while doing it.

3. The Supervisor should remain in good ARC with his students at all times while they are performing training activities.

4. The Supervisor at all times must have a high tolerance of stupidity in his students and must be willing to repeat any datum not understood as many times as necessary for the student to understand and acquire reality on the datum.

5. The Supervisor does not have a "case" in his relationship with his students, nor discuss or talk about his personal problems to the students.

6. The Supervisor will, at all times, be a source point of good control and direction to his students.

7. The Supervisor will be able to correlate any part of Scientology to any other part and to livingness over the eight dynamics.

8. The Supervisor should be able to answer any question concerning Scientology by directing the student to the actual source of the data. If a Supervisor cannot answer a particular question, he should always say so, and the Supervisor should always find the answer to the question from the source and tell the student where the answer is to be found.

9. The Supervisor should never lie to, deceive or misdirect a student concerning Scientology. He shall be honest at all times about it with a student.

10. The Supervisor must be an accomplished auditor.

11. The Supervisor should always set a good example to his students: such as giving good demonstrations, being on time and dressing neatly.

12. The Supervisor should at all times be perfectly willing and able to do anything he tells his students to do.

13. The Supervisor must not become emotionally involved with students of either sex while they are under his or her training.

14. When a Supervisor makes any mistake, he is to inform the student that he has made one and rectify[1] it immediately. This datum embraces all phases in training, demonstrations, lectures and processing, etc. He is never to hide the fact that he made the mistake.

15. The Supervisor should never neglect to give praise to his students when due.

---

1. **rectify:** put or set right; correct.

16. The Supervisor to some degree should be pan-determined about the Supervisor–student relationship.

17. When a Supervisor lets a student control, give orders to or handle the Supervisor in any way for the purpose of demonstration or other training purposes, the Supervisor should always put the student back under his control.

18. The Supervisor will at all times observe the Auditor's Code during sessions and the Code of a Scientologist at all times.

19. The Supervisor will never give a student opinions about Scientology without labeling them thoroughly as such; otherwise, he is to direct only to tested and proven data concerning Scientology.

20. The Supervisor shall never use a student for his own personal gain.

21. The Supervisor will be a stable terminal, point the way to stable data, be certain, but not dogmatic[2] or dictatorial,[3] toward his students.

22. The Supervisor will keep himself at all times informed of the most recent Scientology data and procedures and communicate this information to his students.

---

2. **dogmatic:** characterized by the assertion of opinions in an authoritative or arrogant manner.

3. **dictatorial:** of, like or characteristic of a dictator; domineering.

Supervisor's Stable Data

[1962]

In addition to the Supervisor's Code, there is a primary stable datum about all supervision:

Get the student to accomplish auditing for the preclear and then get the student to accomplish it with better form, speed and accuracy.

A Supervisor must never lose sight of the *purpose* of auditing. Auditing is for the preclear, is intended to improve the preclear's case. Auditing is not just a matter of good form.

The reason some students do not accomplish auditing is that they become so oriented on form alone that they forget the purpose of the form.

Good auditing form and correct sessioning obtain many times the result of bad form and incorrect sessioning. But total form and no effort to do something for the pc results in no auditing.

The result comes before the form in importance. Because students may use this idea to excuse lack of form, Q-and-Aing,[1] and to squirrel[2] with their processes, the stable datum becomes unpopular with Supervisors.

A student should first be held responsible for the state of the pc during and after sessions and made to know that as an auditor he is there to get a fast, good result. The student should then be taught that he can get a better, faster result with better form. After that, the student should be taught that Scientology results are only obtained by correct and exact duplication of Scientology processes, not by offbeat variations.

The student wants to know how to do this or that. Refer him to his materials on how to do the most fundamental actions, but MAKE HIM OR HER *DO* IT. And keep up a running refrain that you want results, results, results, on his pc.

The student will be all thumbs[3] and faint. The Supervisor may be horrified by the goofs. But don't bother with the goofs. Just demand results on the pc, results on the pc, results on the pc.

This action by the Supervisor will teach the student (a) that he or she is supposed to get results in auditing and (b) that results can be obtained and (c) that he or she sure needs better skill.

---

1. **Q-and-Aing:** asking a question about a pc's answer, i.e., the auditor asks a question, the pc answers, the auditor asks a question about the answer. This is the chief auditor fault, as it is giving session control over to the pc. The auditor following only the pc's lead is giving no auditing and the pc is left on "self-audit." Here is a wrong example of auditing: *Auditor:* "How are you?" *Pc:* "Awful." *Auditor:* "What's wrong?" Here is a right example: *Auditor:* "How are you?" *Pc:* "Awful." *Auditor:* "Thank you."

2. **squirrel:** alter Scientology; indulge in offbeat practices.

3. **all thumbs:** clumsy, fumbling.

So the first address in training is to teach those above three things, (a), (b) and (c).

You can't teach a student who doesn't realize that results in the pc depend on the auditor and auditing and that results are *expected* from auditing, who believes results can't be obtained from auditing or wants to prove auditing doesn't work, and who doesn't yet know that he or she doesn't know. *These* are the barriers to training a good auditor.

The gradient approach to the mind is vital. Clearing will not occur without it. But the gradient approach to auditing can be overdone to a point where the student completely loses sight of why he is auditing.

1. First and foremost, the auditor *accomplishes* something for the pc, and without that there is neither sense nor purpose to auditing;

2. Excellent form accomplishes more for the pc faster; and

3. Exact duplication of processes alone returns standard high-level results on all pcs.

The student thrown in over his head learns

A. Results in the pc depend on the auditor and auditing, and that results are expected from auditing;

B. That results *can* be obtained in auditing, and the better the form and duplication, the better the results; and

C. That the student has more to learn about auditing and that the student doesn't yet know.

Therefore, the Supervisor must teach the student

a.   That he or she is supposed to get results in auditing;

b.   That Scientology can obtain results; and

c.   That better form and duplication obtain better, faster results.

I dare say many students learn things just because they are told to and find no relationship between form, duplication and the preclear. Let them fall on their heads and yet obtain results and this attitude will change—and you'll save us a lot of offbeat nonsense and case failures in orgs and the field.

The Credo[1] of a True Group Member

[1951]

1. The successful participant of a group is that participant who closely approximates in his own activities the ideal, ethic and rationale[2] of the overall group.

2. The responsibility of the individual for the group as a whole should not be less than the responsibility of the group for the individual.

3. The group member has, as part of his responsibility, the smooth operation of the entire group.

4. A group member must exert and insist upon his rights and prerogatives[3] as a group member and insist upon the rights and prerogatives of the group as a group and let not these rights be diminished in any way or degree for any excuse or claimed expeditiousness.[4]

5. The member of a true group must exert and practice his right to contribute to the group. And he must insist upon

---

1. **credo:** any creed or formula of belief.
2. **rationale:** the fundamental reasons for something; logical basis.
3. **prerogatives:** exclusive rights or privileges held by a person or group.
4. **expeditiousness:** the quality or state of being prompt and efficient.

the right of the group to contribute to him. He should recognize that a myriad[5] of group failures will result when either of these contributions is denied as a right. (A welfare state being that state in which the member is not permitted to contribute to the state but must take contribution from the state.)

6. Enturbulence of the affairs of the group by sudden shifts of plans unjustified by circumstances, breakdown of recognized channels or cessation of useful operations in a group must be refused and blocked by the member of a group. He should take care not to enturbulate a manager and thus lower ARC.

7. Failure in planning or failure to recognize goals must be corrected by the group member for the group by calling the matter to conference or acting upon his own initiative.

8. A group member must coordinate his initiative with the goals and rationale of the entire group and with other individual members, well publishing his activities and intentions so that all conflicts may be brought forth in advance.

9. A group member must insist upon his right to have initiative.

10. A group member must study and understand and work with the goals, rationale and executions of the group.

11. A group member must work toward becoming as expert as possible in his specialized technology and skill in the group and must assist other individuals of the group to an understanding of that technology and skill and its place in the organizational necessities of the group.

---

5. **myriad:** any indefinitely large number.

12. A group member should have a working knowledge of all technologies and skills in the group in order to understand them and their place in the organizational necessities of the group.

13. On the group member depends the height of the ARC of the group. He must insist upon high-level communication lines and clarity in affinity and reality and know the consequence of not having such conditions. *And he must work continually and actively to maintain high ARC in the organization.*

14. A group member has the right of pride in his tasks and a right of judgment and handling in those tasks.

15. A group member must recognize that he is himself a manager of some section of the group and/or its tasks and that he himself must have both the knowledge and right of management in that sphere for which he is responsible.

16. The group member should not permit laws to be passed which limit or proscribe[6] the activities of all the members of the group because of the failure of some of the members of the group.

17. The group member should insist on flexible planning and unerring execution of plans.

18. The performance of duty at optimum by every member of the group should be understood by the group member to be the best safeguard of his own and the group survival. It is the pertinent business of any member of the group that optimum performance be achieved by any other member of the group whether chain of command or similarity of activity sphere warrants[7] such supervision or not.

---

6. **proscribe:** prohibit as wrong or dangerous; condemn.

7. **warrants:** serves as a justification or reasonable grounds for.

The Credo of a Good and Skilled Manager

[1951]

To be effective and successful a manager must:

1. Understand as fully as possible the goals and aims of the group he manages. He must be able to see and embrace the *ideal* attainment of the goal as envisioned by a goal maker. He must be able to tolerate and better the *practical* attainments and advances of which his group and its members may be capable. He must strive to narrow, always, the ever-existing gulf between the *ideal* and the *practical*.

2. He must realize that a primary mission is the full and honest interpretation by himself of the ideal and ethic and their goals and aims to his subordinates and the group itself. He must lead creatively and persuasively toward these goals his subordinates, the group itself and the individuals of the group.

3. He must embrace the organization and act solely for the entire organization and never form or favor cliques.[1] His judgment of individuals of the group should be solely in the light of their worth to the entire group.

---

1. **cliques:** small, exclusive groups.

4. He must never falter in sacrificing individuals to the good of the group both in planning and execution and in his justice.

5. He must protect all established communication lines and complement them where necessary.

6. He must protect all affinity in his charge and have himself an affinity for the group itself.

7. He must attain always to the highest creative reality.

8. His planning must accomplish, in the light of goals and aims, the activity of the entire group. He must never let organizations grow and sprawl but, learning by pilots, must keep organizational planning fresh and flexible.

9. He must recognize in himself the rationale of the group and receive and evaluate the data out of which he makes his solutions with the highest attention to the truth of that data.

10. He must constitute himself on the orders of service to the group.

11. He must permit himself to be served well as to his individual requirements, practicing an economy of his own efforts and enjoying certain comforts to the wealth of keeping high his rationale.

12. He should require of his subordinates that they relay into their own spheres of management the whole and entire of his true feelings and the reasons for his decisions as clearly as they can be relayed and expanded and interpreted only for the greater understanding of the individuals governed by those subordinates.

13. He must never permit himself to pervert or mask any portion of the ideal and ethic on which the group operates nor must he permit the ideal and ethic to grow old and outmoded and unworkable. He must never permit his planning to be perverted or censored by subordinates. He must never permit the ideal and ethic of the group's individual members to deteriorate, using always reason to interrupt such a deterioration.

14. He must have faith in the goals, faith in himself and faith in the group.

15. He must lead by demonstrating always creative and constructive subgoals. He must not drive by threat and fear.

16. He must realize that every individual in the group is engaged in some degree in the managing of other men, life and MEST and that a liberty of management within this code should be allowed to every such submanager.

Thus conducting himself, a manager can win empire for his group, whatever that empire may be.

12

The
Code of Honor

12

The
Code of Honor

[1952]

No one expects the Code of Honor to be closely and tightly followed.

An ethical code[1] cannot be enforced. Any effort to enforce the Code of Honor would bring it into the level of a moral code.[2] It cannot be enforced simply because it is a way of life which can exist as a way of life only as long as it is not enforced. Any other use but self-determined use of the Code of Honor would, as any Scientologist could quickly see, produce a considerable deterioration in a person. Therefore its use is a luxury use, and which is done solely on self-determined action, providing one sees eye to eye[3] with the Code of Honor.

If you believed man was worthy enough to be granted by you sufficient stature so as to permit you to exercise gladly the Code of Honor, I can guarantee that you would be a happy

---

1. **ethical code:** a code of certain restrictions indulged in to better the manner of conduct of life. A person conducts himself according to such a code because he wants to or because he feels he is proud enough or decent enough or civilized enough to so conduct himself.

2. **moral code:** a series of agreements to which a person has subscribed (agreed, consented) to guarantee the survival of a group.

3. **sees eye to eye:** has exactly the same opinion; agrees.

---

person. And if you found an occasional miscreant[4] falling away from the best standards you have developed, you yet did not turn away from the rest of man, and if you discovered yourself betrayed by those you were seeking to defend and yet did not then experience a complete reversal of opinion about all your fellow men, there would be no dwindling spiral for you.

1. *Never desert a comrade in need, in danger or in trouble.*

2. *Never withdraw allegiance once granted.*

3. *Never desert a group to which you owe your support.*

4. *Never disparage yourself or minimize your strength or power.*

5. *Never need praise, approval or sympathy.*

6. *Never compromise with your own reality.*

7. *Never permit your affinity to be alloyed.[5]*

8. *Do not give or receive communication unless you yourself desire it.*

9. *Your self-determinism and your honor are more important than your immediate life.*

10. *Your integrity to yourself is more important than your body.*

---

4. **miscreant:** an evil person; criminal; villain.

5. **alloyed:** weakened or spoiled through the addition of something that reduces value or pleasure.

11. *Never regret yesterday. Life is in you today, and you make your tomorrow.*

12. *Never fear to hurt another in a just cause.*

13. *Don't desire to be liked or admired.*

14. *Be your own adviser, keep your own counsel[6] and select your own decisions.*

15. *Be true to your own goals.*

---

6. **counsel:** that in which deliberation results; resolution; purpose; intention; plan.

13

The Creed
of the Church
of Scientology

13

The Creed of the Church of Scientology

[1954]

We of the Church believe:

That all men of whatever race, color or creed were created with equal rights;

That all men have inalienable[1] rights to their own religious practices and their performance;

That all men have inalienable rights to their own lives;

That all men have inalienable rights to their sanity;

That all men have inalienable rights to their own defense;

That all men have inalienable rights to conceive, choose, assist or support their own organizations, churches and governments;

That all men have inalienable rights to think freely, to talk freely, to write freely their own opinions and to counter or utter or write upon the opinions of others;

That all men have inalienable rights to the creation of their own kind;

---

1. **inalienable:** that may not be taken away or transferred.

That the souls of men have the rights of men;

That the study of the mind and the healing of mentally caused ills should not be alienated[2] from religion or condoned[3] in non-religious fields;

And that no agency less than God has the power to suspend or set aside these rights, overtly or covertly.

And we of the Church believe:

That man is basically good;

That he is seeking to survive;

That his survival depends upon himself and upon his fellows and his attainment of brotherhood with the universe.

And we of the Church believe that the laws of God forbid man:

To destroy his own kind;

To destroy the sanity of another;

To destroy or enslave another's soul;

To destroy or reduce the survival of one's companions or one's group.

And we of the Church believe that the spirit can be saved and that the spirit alone may save or heal the body.

---

2. **alienated:** withdrawn or detached from.

3. **condoned:** given tacit (implied or unspoken) approval.

About the Author

About the Author

Exploration and adventure were a way of life for L. Ron Hubbard. He traveled the world, observing firsthand the different customs and practices of a multitude of cultures.

As Ron said, "One doesn't learn about life by sitting in an ivory tower, thinking about it. One learns about life by being part of it." And that is how he lived.

Born in Tilden, Nebraska on 13 March 1911, his life was anything but sheltered. He was brought up in the rough environment of Montana where he learned very quickly that survival depended utterly on personal ability.

In his early teens, Ron traveled extensively. By the age of nineteen he had traveled a quarter of a million miles, including voyages to China, Japan and other points in the Orient and South Pacific, and had become closely acquainted with twenty-one different races in areas all over the world.

After returning to the United States, he attended George Washington University, where he studied engineering, higher mathematics and was even a member of one of the first American classes in nuclear physics ever taught.

Throughout his travels, his formal studies and his own professional activities, Ron never deviated from his primary purpose of providing mankind with a workable technology to improve life. He had realized that there *was* no real technology of the human mind and found that the "technologies" which mental practitioners had evolved on this planet were in fact barbarisms. He was determined to find a solution to this through his studies of mankind and life.

The results of his research were first made known in the book *The Dynamics of Life*, written in 1948, which was copied and passed from hand to hand. As copies of the manuscript circulated, Ron began to receive a steadily increasing flow of letters asking for further information and more applications of his new subject. He soon found he was spending all his time answering letters and decided to write a comprehensive text on the subject.

With the publication of *Dianetics: The Modern Science of Mental Health* in May 1950, the exact fundamental axioms and procedures of the technology of Dianetics were made broadly available for the first time. This easily understood and workable technology of the mind spread like wildfire, and the book *Dianetics* continues to be immensely popular with people from all walks of life to this day.

Following the release of this phenomenal bestseller, Ron was in even greater demand for lectures, demonstrations and further information on Dianetics. But his explorations and continuing research led him further and further into the realm of the human spirit. Breakthrough after breakthrough followed, each pushing aside previously insurmountable barriers and opening up new vistas of existence. With the development of Scientology philosophy and technology in the early 1950s, Ron moved fully into the field of freeing the spirit of man, discovering and devising exact, workable procedures for smoothing the way to total spiritual freedom.

In three decades of research and development, Ron isolated and recorded the exact stable data of all his discoveries. These were the primary axioms and postulates which formed the basis of all formulas and procedures in Dianetics and Scientology.

In 1970, many of these major fundamental data and principles were assembled into *Scientology 0-8: The Book of Basics*, which has become an invaluable reference text and handbook for professional auditors and students alike.

Ron dedicated his life to helping others and to developing techniques that would ensure the route to a higher level of understanding could be traveled by anyone.

His works—including an astounding number of books, taped lectures, instructional films, writings, demonstrations and briefings—are studied and applied in hundreds of Dianetics and Scientology organizations all over the world. Additionally, millions of individuals spanning every continent apply his technology daily to improve their lives.

With his research fully completed and codified, L. Ron Hubbard departed his body on 24 January 1986.

The spiritual technology he has given mankind makes it possible for us to achieve Ron's dream, "A civilization without insanity, without criminals and without war, where the able can prosper and honest beings can have rights, and where man is free to rise to greater heights."

His works make this dream attainable. Applying his technology is all that is needed to achieve it.

Glossary

aberration: a departure from rational thought or behavior. From the Latin, *aberrare,* to wander from; Latin, *ab,* away, *errare,* to wander. It means basically to err, to make mistakes, or more specifically to have fixed ideas which are not true. Aberration is opposed to sanity, which would be its opposite.

abstract: theoretical rather than practical.

Academy: the part of a Scientology church in which auditing courses and training are delivered.

action phrases: words or phrases in engrams or locks which cause the individual to perform involuntary actions on the time track.

adherence: the action of remaining faithful to or continuing to support.

adhesion: *(physics)* the force that holds together the molecules of unlike substances whose surfaces are in contact: distinguished from cohesion. *See also* **cohesion** in this glossary.

advocate: to speak or write in support of; be in favor of.

aesthetic: *(adj.)* having the nature of a wavelength closely resembling theta or a harmony approximating theta; beautiful.

aggregations: masses formed by the union of distinct particles; gatherings, assemblages, collections.

alienated: withdrawn or detached from.

alloyed: weakened or spoiled through the addition of something that reduces value or pleasure.

all thumbs: clumsy, fumbling.

aloof: at a distance, especially in feeling or interest; apart.

analyzer: the analytical mind: that portion of the mind which perceives and retains experience data to compose and resolve problems.

anchor points: dimension points which demark the outermost boundaries of a space or its corners. Anchor points, along with the viewpoint, are responsible for space. An anchor point is a dimension point that stays rather still, to keep the space created.

apparency: that which appears to be, as distinct from what actually is.

applicative: applying or capable of being applied, as to some practical use.

arbitrary: something which is introduced into a situation without regard to the data of the situation.

ARC break: a sudden drop or cutting of one's affinity, reality or communication with someone or something. Upsets with people or things come about because of a lessening or sundering of affinity, reality, or communication or understanding. It's called an ARC break instead of an upset because if one discovers which of the three points of understanding have been cut, one can bring about a rapid recovery in the person's state of mind.

assessment: an inventory and evaluation of a preclear, his body and his case to establish processing level and procedure.

assist: a simple, easily done process that can be applied to anyone to help them recover more rapidly from accidents, mild illness or upsets; any process which assists the individual to heal himself or be healed by another agency by removing his reasons for precipitating (bringing on) and prolonging his condition and lessening his predisposition (inclination or tendency) to further injure himself or remain in an intolerable condition.

associative: tending to connect, bring into relation or unite.

attenuated: weakened; reduced in force or in value.

Audited NOTs: *NOTs* is short for *New Era Dianetics for OTs,* a pre-OT level consisting of a series of confidential rundowns delivered by a specially trained OT auditor. Some of the mysteries of life have been exposed to full view for the first time ever in NOTs.

auditor: a person trained and qualified in applying Dianetics and/or Scientology processes and procedures to individuals for their betterment; called an auditor because *auditor* means "one who listens."

Auschwitz: city in southwest Poland; site of a Nazi concentration camp notorious as an extermination center.

authoritative: having the support or weight of authority; accepted by most authorities in a field.

awry: wrong; amiss.

axioms: statements of natural laws on the order of those of the physical sciences.

bank: *see* **engram bank** in this glossary.

beingness: the assumption or choosing of a category of identity. Beingness is assumed by oneself or given to oneself or is attained. Examples of beingness would be one's own name, one's profession, one's physical characteristics, one's role in a game — each and all of these could be called one's beingness.

Belsen: village in West Germany; the site of a Nazi concentration camp and extermination center.

black or invisible field: some part of a mental image picture where the preclear is looking at blackness or invisibility. It is part of some lock, secondary or engram that is black or invisible.

blue, bolt from the: a sudden, unforeseen occurrence.

cabal: a secret scheme; plot.

case(s): a general term for a person being treated or helped. It also refers to his condition, which is monitored by the content of his reactive mind. A person's case is the way he responds to the world around him by reason of his aberrations.

case gain: the improvements and resurgences a person experiences from auditing; any case betterment according to the pc.

case supervision: referring to the actions of the Case Supervisor. The C/S is the auditor's "handler." He tells the auditor what to do, keeps him corrected, keeps the lines straight and keeps the auditor calm and willing and winning. The C/S directs what auditing actions are done for each individual preclear under his care. All case supervision is for the benefit of the preclear. *See also* **case(s)** in this glossary.

catatonia: a very fancy word denoting a state in which a person is still, stiff and never moves.

characteristics: distinguishing traits, features or qualities.

chemical-heat engine: a mechanism for converting chemical energy (from food or other fuel) into heat energy and mechanical energy; a body.

chronic: constant; habitual.

Claims Verification Board: an official group within the Church of Scientology which facilitates refund requests.

Clear: the name of a state achieved through auditing, or an individual who has achieved this state. A Clear is a being who no longer has his own reactive mind. A Clear is an unaberrated person and is rational in that he forms the best possible solutions he can on the data he has and from his viewpoint. The Clear has no engrams which can be restimulated to throw out the correctness of computation by entering hidden and false data.

cliques: small, exclusive groups.

cohesion: the force by which the molecules of a substance are held together: distinguished from adhesion. *See also* **adhesion** in this glossary.

coma: a state of deep and prolonged unconsciousness caused by injury or disease.

comm, cut his: cut (stopped, halted) his communication.

common denominator: a quality, opinion or other attribute shared by all the persons or things in a group.

condoned: given tacit (implied or unspoken) approval.

conjunction: combination; union.

consideration: thinking, believing, supposing, postulating. Consideration is the highest capability of life, taking rank over the mechanics of space, energy and time.

corollary: a natural consequence or result; something that follows logically after something else is proved.

counsel: that in which deliberation results; resolution; purpose; intention; plan.

counter-efforts: the efforts of the environment (physical) against the individual. The individual's own effort is simply called effort. The efforts of the environment are called counter-efforts.

credo: any creed or formula of belief.

creed: a statement of belief, principles or opinions on any subject; a brief statement of religious belief.

critical: tending to find fault.

culminated: ended or arrived at a final stage.

deaberrating: removing aberration. *See also* **aberration** in this glossary.

decried: spoken out against strongly and openly; denounced.

deduced: inferred from a general rule or principle; reached (a conclusion) by reasoning.

delineates: describes in words; portrays.

derive: draw or form.

Dewey: John Dewey (1859–1952), American philosopher and educator.

Dharma: a body of scientific-philosophical-religious truth, written about 600 B.C. The Dharma rose up in Asia and its doctrines were spread to hundreds of millions of people by Gautama Buddha. Dharma was the name of a legendary Hindu sage—a mythological figure. The word means *knowingness* or *lookingness*.

dictatorial: of, like or characteristic of a dictator; domineering.

differentiative: having to do with the ability to "tell the difference" between one person and another, one object and another.

dimension: the distance from the point of view to the anchor point that is in space; a measure of spatial extent, especially width, height or length.

diverge: to depart from a given viewpoint, practice, etc.; differ.

divulged: made known; disclosed; revealed.

dogmatic: characterized by the assertion of opinions in an authoritative or arrogant manner.

drop (on the meter): a dip of the E-Meter needle to the right as you face the meter. Also called a fall, the most used and observed needle action. It means to the auditor "I've found it" or "I've gotten a response in the bank."

duality: the condition or fact of being dual, or consisting of two parts, natures, etc.; twofold condition.

dub-in: any unknowingly created mental picture that appears to have been a record of the physical universe but is, in fact, only an altered copy of the time track. It is a phrase out of the motion-picture industry of putting a sound track on top of something that isn't there.

dwindling spiral: a phenomenon of the ARC triangle whereby when one breaks some affinity, a little bit of the reality goes down, and then communication goes down, which makes it impossible to get affinity as high as before; so a little bit more gets knocked off affinity, and then reality goes down, and then communication. This is the dwindling spiral in progress, until it hits the bottom—death—which is no affinity, no communication and no reality.

dynamic: of or relating to the motivating or driving force, physical or moral, in any field.

E-Meter: an electronic device for measuring the mental state or change of state of *Homo sapiens*. It is *not* a lie detector. It does not diagnose or cure anything. It is used by auditors to assist the preclear in locating areas of spiritual distress or travail.

emotingness: the condition of having or manifesting emotion.

endocrine: of or relating to the endocrine system, a group of glands which secrete hormones directly into the bloodstream which influence or regulate other organs in the body.

engram bank: the reactive mind, that portion of the mind which works on a stimulus-response basis (given a certain stimulus it will automatically give a certain response) which is not under a person's volitional control and which exerts force and power over a person's awareness, purposes, thoughts, body and actions. It consists of locks, secondaries, engrams and chains of them and is the single source of human aberration and psychosomatic ills.

ensuing: following immediately.

entheta lines: communication lines which are slanderous, choppy or destructive in an attempt to overwhelm or suppress a person or group. *Entheta* is short for enturbulated theta (thought or life).

entities: beings; existences.

enturbulence: turbulence; agitation; disturbance.

eradicating: getting rid of; wiping out; destroying.

esoteric: intended only for people with special knowledge or interest.

ethical code: a code of certain restrictions indulged in to better the manner of conduct of life. A person conducts himself according to such a code because he wants to or because he feels he is proud enough or decent enough or civilized enough to so conduct himself.

evaluate: to impose data or knowledge upon another. An example would be to tell another why he is the way he is instead of permitting or guiding him to discover it for himself.

evolved: developed or worked out gradually.

Expanded Lower Grades: each Grade is a series of processes which are run on a preclear with the purpose of bringing him to a particular state of Release. These are called "expanded" because they use all the processes of the level developed between 1950 and 1970 and are run on all four flows. The Expanded Lower Grades include Expanded ARC Straightwire through Expanded Lower Grade IV, as given in the Chart of Abilities Gained.

expeditiousness: the quality or state of being prompt and efficient.

eye to eye, sees: has exactly the same opinion; agrees.

facsimiles: three-dimensional color pictures with sound and smell and all other perceptions, plus the conclusions or speculations of the individual.

finite: having bounds or limits; not infinite; measurable.

fixidity: rigid or immobile; stationary or unchanging in relative position; fixed.

floating needle: the same as a free needle. *See* **free needle** in this glossary.

flow: a directional thought, energy or action. The four flows referred to in the Chart of Abilities Gained are: Flow 1, something happening to self; Flow 2, doing something to another; Flow 3, others doing things to others; Flow 0, self doing something to self.

flying of ruds: the addressing (taking up) and handling of rudiments (those steps or actions used to get the pc in shape to be audited) by taking his attention off any current upsets or worries or other distractions that might make it difficult for him to be audited.

formula: a rule or method for doing something.

40.0: *see* **Tone Scale in Full** in the Scales section of this book.

free needle: the same as a floating needle (F/N), which is a rhythmic sweep of the E-Meter dial at a slow, even pace of the needle, back and forth, back and forth, without change in the width of the swing except perhaps to widen as the pc gets off the last small bits of charge (harmful energy or force). A free needle or floating needle is one of the parts of the end phenomena (process completion) for any process or action.

furtherance: the act of furthering; advancement.

games conditions: the factors which make a game, which is a contest of person against person or team against team. A game consists of freedoms, barriers and purposes, and there is a necessity in a game to have an opponent or an enemy. Also there is a necessity to have problems, and enough individuality to cope with a situation. To live life fully, then, one must have in addition to "something to do," a higher purpose, and this purpose, to be a purpose at all, must have counter-purposes or purposes which prevent it from occurring. This last is very important: If a person lacks problems, opponents and counter-purposes to his own, he will invent them. Here we have in essence the totality of aberration.

Gautama Buddha: (563–483 B.C.) originally Gautama Sakyamuni, founder of the Buddhist religion. The term *Buddha* derives from *Bodhi,* or "one who has attained intellectual and ethical perfection by human means."

GE: the genetic entity. It is that beingness not dissimilar to the thetan that has carried forward and developed the body from its earliest moments along the evolutionary line on Earth and which, through experience, necessity and natural selection, has employed the counter-efforts of the environment to fashion an organism of the type best fitted for survival, limited only by the abilities of the GE. The goal of the GE is survival on a much grosser plane of materiality (concerning the material or physical).

Grades: each Grade is a series of processes which are run on a preclear with the purpose of bringing him to a particular state of Release. The Grades encompass Expanded ARC Straightwire, Expanded Lower Grades 0–IV, Grade V, Grade VA and Grade VI. *See also* **Expanded Lower Grades** in this glossary.

graduated scale: (also called a *gradient scale*) a scale of condition graduated from zero to infinity. On a scale of survival, everything above zero or center would be more and more survival, approaching an infinite survival (immortality), and everything below zero or center would be more and more nonsurvival, approaching an infinite nonsurvival (death). Absolutes are considered to be unobtainable.

gravitic: of or having to do with weight or heaviness.

group processes: auditing techniques administered to groups of children or adults by a group auditor.

harmonious: agreeably related; in accord.

hazardings: offerings of statements, conjectures, etc.

hitherto: up to this time; until now.

Hubbard Solo NOTs Auditing Course: the course which covers the materials necessary to be able to audit Solo NOTs, New OT VI. *See also* **Solo NOTs** in this glossary.

humanities: the branches of learning concerned with human thought and relations, as distinguished from the sciences; especially literature, philosophy, history, etc.

hysteria: an extreme degree of emotional instability.

ideal scene: how something ought to be. The entire concept of an ideal scene is a clean statement of its purpose.

ill effects: harmful, bad or unfavorable consequences, developments or results.

impinged: struck, hit or dashed (on, upon or against something).

imponderable, an: something which cannot be conclusively determined or explained.

inalienable: that may not be taken away or transferred.

inception: beginning; start.

incursion: a running, bringing or entering in or into, with vigorous, forceful or determined effort.

individuation: 1. formation into an individual; development as a separate organic (living) unit. 2. a withdrawal out of groups and into only self. The mechanics of individuation are first, communication into, and then refusal to communicate into.

induced: reasoned in such a way as to produce general laws through known facts.

inductive: of or relating to induction, a way of reasoning using known facts to produce general laws.

ingression: the action of entering; entrance.

inherently: in itself or oneself; by its or one's nature.

initiative: the characteristic of originating new ideas or methods; ability to think and act without being urged; enterprise.

inkling: hint; a slight knowledge or suspicion.

integrating: putting or bringing (parts) together into a whole; unifying.

integrity: adherence to moral and ethical principles; soundness of moral character; honesty. It comes from the Latin word *integritas*, meaning untouched, undivided, whole.

intermediate: being, situated or acting between two points.

interpose: to be or come between.

intervene: to come between as an influencing force, as in order to modify, settle or hinder some action, argument, etc.

introversion: a looking in too closely; having one's attention and interest directed upon oneself.

inversion: a switch to an opposite obsessive consideration, such as from compulsion to inhibition.

ivory tower: figuratively, a place of mental withdrawal from reality and action.

Kant: Immanuel Kant (1724–1804), German philosopher; sought to determine laws and limits of man's knowledge.

kinesthesia: the sensation of position, movement, tension, etc., of parts of the body.

lamaseries: monasteries of the lamas (Buddhist monks of Tibet and Mongolia).

latent: not visible or apparent; hidden; dormant.

Life Repair: a series of auditing actions run on a preclear who is starting out in auditing for the first time. Life Repair would address such things as rough spots in life, periods which the preclear may feel bad about, areas of overwhelm, etc.

lines: referring to communication lines, the routes along which communications travel from one person to another; the lines on which particles flow.

livingness: the activity of going along a certain course, impelled (driven) by a purpose and with some place to arrive.

locks: mental image pictures of non-painful but disturbing experiences the person has experienced and which depend for their force on earlier secondaries and engrams which the experiences have restimulated (stirred up).

Logics: a method of thinking. They apply to any universe or any thinking process. They are the forms of thought behavior which can, but do not necessarily have to, be used in creating universes.

machine: an actual machine in the mind (like ordinary machinery), constructed out of mental mass and energy, that has been made by the individual to do work for him, usually having been set up so as to come into operation automatically under certain predetermined circumstances.

magnitude: greatness of size, extent, importance or influence.

make-guilty: the action of a person excusing or making his own actions right by making another or others wrong or quilty. It is a mechanism used to dominate or escape domination and enhance one person's survival and injure that of another.

make the grade: overcome obstacles and succeed.

maligned: spoken evilly of; slandered.

materialistic: of or concerning materialism, the opinion that only physical matter exists.

maximal: the highest or greatest possible.

mechanics: referring to space, energy, objects and time. When something has those things in it, it constitutes something mechanical.

methodologies: systems of methods and procedures.

miscreant: an evil person; criminal; villain.

Montgomery, Field Marshal: Sir Bernard Law Montgomery (1887–1976), British field marshal in World War II. He commanded the British army which drove the Germans out of Egypt and was later the commander of the Allied armies in Northern France. Made chief of the British general staff in 1946. [*Field marshal:* an officer next in rank to the commander in chief in the British, French, German and some other armies.]

moral code: a series of agreements to which a person has subscribed (agreed, consented) to guarantee the survival of a group.

motivator: that thing which moves, rouses, urges on.

motor: causing or producing motion.

myriad: any indefinitely large number.

nebulous: unclear, vague or indefinite.

negligible: so small or unimportant that it may safely be neglected or disregarded.

neurological: having to do with the nervous system, its structure and diseases.

neurosis: a condition wherein a person is insane or disturbed on some subject (as opposed to psychosis, wherein a person is just insane in general).

New Era Dianetics: a summary and refinement of Dianetics based upon thirty years of experience in the application of the subject. New Era Dianetics was released in 1978 and

New Era Dianetics auditing and training are today available in all Scientology organizations.

Nietzsche: Friedrich Wilhelm Nietzsche (1844–1900), German philosopher and poet. He denounced all religion and promoted the "morals of masters," the doctrine of perfecting man through forcible self-assertion and glorification of the "superman." His theories are regarded as having influenced the German attitudes in World War I and the Nazi regime.

no-games condition: a totality of barriers or a totality of freedom. *See also* **games conditions** in this glossary.

NOTs: New Era Dianetics for OTs.

novel: of a new kind.

Objectives: Objective Processes. *Objective* refers to outward things, not the thoughts or feelings of the individual. Objective Processes deal with the real and observable. They call for the preclear to spot or find something exterior to himself in order to carry out the auditing command. Objectives locate the person in his environment, establish direct communication with the auditor, and they bring a person to present time, a very important factor in mental and spiritual sanity and ability.

obsessive: of or having to do with an idea, wish, etc., that fills one's thoughts and cannot be put out of the mind by the person.

Occident: the part of the world west of Asia, especially Europe and the Americas.

occlude: hide; make unavailable to conscious recall.

ologies: branches of learning; sciences (a humorous usage).

orgs: *(Scientology slang)* organizations that deliver Dianetics and Scientology training and processing.

Orient: the East; countries east of the Mediterranean, especially East Asia.

orientation: alignment or position with respect to a reference system.

OT: Operating Thetan. It is a state of beingness. It is a being "at cause over matter, energy, space, time, form and life." *Operating* comes from "able to operate without dependency on things," and *Thetan* is the Greek letter theta (θ), which the Greeks used to represent *thought* or perhaps *spirit*, to which an *n* is added to make a noun in the modern style used to create words in engineering. It is also θ^n or "theta to the nth degree," meaning unlimited or vast.

overrun: continue a process or a series of processes past the optimum point.

pan-determinism: the willingness to start, change and stop two or more forces, whether or not opposed, and this could be interpreted as two or more individuals, two or more groups, two or more planets, two or more life-species, two or more universes, two or more spirits, whether or not opposed. This means that one would not necessarily choose sides.

pc: an abbreviation for preclear. *See also* **preclear** in this glossary.

perceptics: sense messages.

phenomena: observable facts or events.

physiology: the vital processes of an organism.

physique: physical or bodily structure, appearance or development.

plastically: flexibly; impressionably.

practitioners: people who practice a profession, art, etc.

precedence: priority in time or order.

preclear: a spiritual being who is now on the road to becoming Clear, hence pre-Clear.

Prelogics: *see* **Qs** in this glossary.

pre-OT: a thetan beyond the state of Clear who, through the pre-OT levels, is advancing to the full state of Operating Thetan (OT). *See also* **pre-OT levels** in this glossary.

pre-OT levels: the advanced auditing levels after Clear and preparatory to the actual OT levels which begin at New OT VIII. The pre-OT levels are New OT I through New OT VII. *See also* **pre-OT** in this glossary.

prerogatives: exclusive rights or privileges held by a person or group.

processes: sets of questions asked or commands given by an auditor to help a person find out things about himself or life and to improve his condition.

processing: the application of Dianetics or Scientology processes to someone by a trained auditor. The exact definition of processing is: The action of asking a preclear a question (which he can understand and answer), getting an answer to that question and acknowledging him for that answer. Also called auditing.

procreation: bringing (a living thing) into existence by the natural process of reproduction; generation.

progeny: offspring; descendants.

propitiate: attempt to appease or buy off some danger or imagined danger.

proscribe: prohibit as wrong or dangerous; condemn.

proximity: nearness.

psychosis: *see* **neurosis** in this glossary.

psychosomatic: *psycho* refers to mind and *somatic* refers to body; the term *psychosomatic* means the mind making the body ill or illnesses which have been created physically within the body by derangement of the mind.

Purif: short for Purification Rundown. *See* **Purification Rundown** in this glossary.

Purification Rundown: a special rundown (series of specific actions done on a case) designed to purify and clean out of one's system the restimulative drug or chemical residues which could act to prevent case gain from Dianetics or Scientology processing.

Q-and-Aing: asking a question about a pc's answer, i.e., the auditor asks a question, the pc answers, the auditor asks a question about the answer. This is the chief auditor fault, as it is giving session control over to the pc. The auditor following only the pc's lead is giving no auditing and the pc is left on "self-audit." Here is a wrong example of auditing: *Auditor:* "How are you?" *Pc:* "Awful." *Auditor:* "What's wrong?" Here is a right example: *Auditor:* "How are you?" *Pc:* "Awful." *Auditor:* "Thank you."

Qs: knowledge is a pyramid, and knowledge as a pyramid has a common denominator which evaluates all other data below it. At the top point of this pyramid is what could be called a Q, and it could also be called a common denominator. It is in common to every other datum in this pyramid full of data. The Qs are the highest echelon from which all other things are derived. Q comes from *quod* in Q.E.D. *(quod erat demonstrandum)*, meaning "which was to be shown or demonstrated," used specifically in mathematical proofs.

rationale: the fundamental reasons for something; a logical basis.

recourse: a turning or seeking for aid, safety, etc.

rectify: put or set right; correct.

rehabilitated: restored to some former ability or state of being or some more optimum condition.

relapse: the act or instance of slipping or falling back into a former condition, especially after improvement.

Release: the term for what occurs when a person separates from his reactive mind or some part of it. The degree and relative permanence of being pulled out of the reactive mind determines the state of Release. There are a number of states or stages of Release and these are called Grades. *See also* **Grades; Expanded Lower Grades** in this glossary.

residual: remaining; left over.

restimulation: reactivation of a past memory due to similar circumstances in the present approximating circumstances of the past.

reticent: habitually silent or uncommunicative; reserved.

revelation: a revealing; the making known of something that was secret or hidden.

rising needle: a needle phenomenon where the needle moves to the auditor's left (auditor facing the meter). It means the preclear has struck an area or something he isn't confronting.

saline content: a sense of the salt content (of the body).

Schopenhauer: Arthur Schopenhauer (1788–1860), German philosopher. He maintained that the desires and drives of men, as well as the forces of nature, are manifestations of a single will, specifically the will to live, which is the essence of the world. Since operation of the will means constant striving without satisfaction, life consists of suffering. Only by controlling the will through the intellect, by suppressing the desire to reproduce, can suffering be diminished.

Scientology Drug Rundown: a rundown (series of auditing actions) which uses Scientology auditing techniques to handle the harmful effects of drugs, medicine and alcohol on a case. This rundown extroverts a person, brings him into present time, and allows him to experience the relief and expansion available to one who has been freed from the influence of drugs.

secondaries: also called *secondary engrams.* Periods of anguish brought about by a major loss or threat of loss to the individual. The secondary engram depends for its strength and force upon physical-pain engrams which underlie it.

self-abasement: a lowering, humiliating or degrading of oneself.

servomechanism: a device which is set in motion by another mechanism and monitors the operation or power of the operating mechanism by the way in which it operates.

session: a precise period of time during which an auditor audits a preclear.

shut-off: something that shuts off a flow or movement.

solid communication line: a communication line is the route along which a communication travels from one person to another; the line on which particles flow. A solid communication line is one requiring solid contact, such as the auditor's hand in the preclear's hand or the preclear's hand in his.

solo: referring to auditing done on advanced levels in Scientology where one is both auditor and pc. Solo auditing occurs in session with an E-Meter.

Solo NOTs: *NOTs* is short for *New Era Dianetics for OTs.* This pre-OT level is audited by the pre-OT solo (meaning audited on oneself). The end phenomena of Solo NOTs is *Cause Over Life.*

species: a group of animals or plants that have certain permanent characteristics in common.

Spencer, Herbert: (1820–1903) English philosopher. He is known for his application of the doctrines of evolution to philosophy and ethics.

sporadic: happening from time to time; not constant or regular.

squirrel: alter Scientology; indulge in offbeat practices.

stage four needle: an E-Meter manifestation in which the needle comes up about an inch or two, and sticks and falls back, and comes up and sticks and falls back (always the same distance). And no matter what one asks the person, he gets a glib explanation. That is the manifestation of the case matched against the manifestation of the needle. A stage four case is not batty; he is simply stuck in a machine.

standard technology: the exact processes and auditing actions laid down by L. Ron Hubbard and used for the invariable resolution of cases, taught in the organizations of Scientology and used without variation by all Scientology auditors. The term applies equally to Dianetics and its technology.

static: 1. not changing. 2. something that has no mass, no location and no position in time, and which has no wavelength at all.

status quo: the existing state of affairs (at a particular time).

stimulus-response: given a certain stimulus something will automatically give a certain response.

subjective: proceeding from or taking place in an individual's mind.

substantiated: supported with evidence; proven.

sundering: breaking or tearing apart; severing.

Sunshine Rundown: a special auditing step done by Clears after they attest to having attained the state of Clear.

symbiotes: any or all life or energy forms which are mutually dependent for survival. The atom depends on the universe, the universe on the atom.

synonymous: equivalent or similar in meaning.

Tao of Lao-tse: the Tao Teh King or Tao Te Ching. The word *Tao* means "the way to solving the mystery which underlies all mysteries." Lao-tse (604–531 B.C.), its author, was one of the great philosophers of China.

tentative: unsure; uncertain; not definite or positive; hesitant.

terminals: things that can receive, relay or send communications (most common usage); also, things with mass and meaning.

thermal: having to do with heat.

theta bop: a small or wide steady dance of the needle. Over a spread of one-eighth of an inch, say (depending on sensitivity setting, it can be half an inch or a whole dial), the needle goes up and down perhaps five or ten times a second. It goes up, sticks, falls, sticks, goes up, sticks, etc., always the same distance, like a slow tuning fork. It is a constant distance and a constant speed, hooking at each end of the swing. A theta bop means "death," "leaving," "don't want to be here."

thetan: what we call the living unit in Scientology. Taken from the Greek letter *theta*, the mathematical symbol used in Scientology to indicate the source of life and life itself. It is the individual, the being; that which is aware of being aware; the identity which is the individual. The thetan is most familiar to one and all as "you."

time track: the consecutive record of mental image pictures which accumulates through a person's life or lives. It is very exactly dated.

Tone Scale: a gradient scale which plots the descending spiral of life from full vitality and consciousness through half-vitality and half-consciousness down to death and the minus tones lying beneath death on the scale. *See also* **Tone Scale in Full** in the Scales section of this book.

toxins: any of various poisonous compounds produced by some microorganisms and causing certain diseases.

transiently: fleetingly; temporarily; briefly.

unmock: become nothing.

unto: a compound of *un* (on) and *to*. It is simply an obsolete form of "to," and is mainly used as a poetic device or for effect.

unwarranted: not justified; unreasonable.

valences: personalities. The term is used to denote the borrowing of the personalities of others. Valences are substitutes for self taken on after the fact of lost confidence in self. Pre-clears "in their father's valence" are acting as though they were their father.

vanquish: overcome.

vaporings: instances or occurrences of vapor, a gaseous form of any substance which is usually a liquid or a solid.

vector: a physical quantity with both magnitude and direction, such as a force or velocity.

Veda: the most ancient sacred writings of the Hindus.

viewpoint: a point of awareness from which one can perceive.

volitional: of or having to do with the use of one's own will in choosing or making a decision, etc.

warrants: serves as a justification or reasonable grounds for.

whistling in the dark: trying to be courageous or hopeful in a fearful or trying situation.

whole track: the moment-to-moment record of a person's existence in this universe in picture and impression form.

0.0: *see* **The Tone Scale in Full** in the Scales section of this book.

Index

case gain,
flying of ruds, more gain than
ten years of
psychoanalysis, 173
six divisions of, 174–75
cause, hallucinatory cause, 146,
151
CDEI Scale, 125–26
inverted, 125
certainty, knowledge is certainty,
not data, 103
Character, New OT X, 186
charge, defined, 155
Chart of Abilities Gained, 179–86
Chart of Attitudes, top and bottom
buttons, 135
Chart of Human Evaluation,
emotion section of Know to
Mystery Scale, 87
Claims Verification Board, 193
Clear(s), 174, 184
alternate Clear route, 184
From Clear to Eternity, 173–78
Clearing Course, 184
code(s),
Auditor's Code, 191–94
Code of Honor, 213–15
Credo of a Good and Skilled
Manager, 207–9
Credo of a True Group Member,
203–4
Scientologist, Code of a, 189–90
Supervisor's Code, 195–97
Supervisor's Stable Data,
199–202
Code of Honor, 213–15
common denominator(s),
all experience, 81
life organisms, motion, 57
of knowledge, Qs, 81
self-determinism, 72
survive, 7
communication, *see also* **ARC**
accomplishes change in MEST, 91
affinity and reality exist to
further, 23, 108

communication, *(cont.)*
ARC, communication is most
important, 23, 108
component parts, 87
defined, 67, 87, 92, 95
depends upon duplication, 96
exact as it approaches
duplication, 96
formula, 87
Release, Expanded Grade 0, 180
scale, 115, 116
solid comm lines, reality level
of, 121
conception, living, death, 137
conclusion(s), defined, 61
conditions of existence,
defined, 84
survival and, 86
Confront Scale, 154
conservatism, effects tolerable on
self, others, 148
consideration(s),
and mechanics, 29–31
freedom to alter considerations,
30
man's inverted view of
importance of, 30
MEST, agreed-upon
considerations, 29
rank over mechanics of space,
energy and time, 29
stupidity, unknownness of
consideration, 89
theta is capable of,
consideration, 91
truth is the exact consideration,
89
control, knowledge, responsibility
and control, 24
coordination within the group, 204
counter-efforts producing action
phrases, 60
covert hostility, effects tolerable on
self, others, 149
creation,
aberration in terms of creation
and destruction, 131–32
as-isness and, 84

mind, *(cont.)*
servomechanism to any
mathematics, 50
theta command post, 57
mixing practices, Auditor's Code
on, 192
Montgomery, Field Marshal, 25
motion,
common denominator of life
organisms, 57
defined, 57
Scale of Motion, 130
time is measured by motion,
158

neurotic, defined, 74
New Era Dianetics,
case completion, 184
Drug Rundown, 184
New OT VIII, Truth Revealed, 185
New OT IX, Orders of Magnitude,
186
New OT X, Character, 186
New OT XI, Operating, 186
New OT XII, Future, 186
Nietzsche, 5
no-games conditions, 138–39
not-isness, defined, 84

Objectives, 179
orientation,
beingness, havingness and
doingness, 93
location, axioms and formula
about, 93
OT levels, 174; *see also* **pre-OT
levels**
OT VIII–XV, 185–86
overrun, Auditor's Code on, 192

pain, defined, 74, 76
pan-determinism,
defined, 129, 141
deterioration into no
responsibility, 129
scale, 141

perceptic(s), list of, 165–67
perception(s),
defined, 69
depends upon duplication, 96
persistence,
admiration, absence alone
permits persistence, 100
defined, 56
governed by strength of basic
dynamic, 35
philosophy,
decry suppression of
knowledge, 190
roots of Scientology, 3
physiology, Behavior and
Physiology Scale, 123
planning, manager, 208
pleasure, reward of survival
activity, 38, 58
Points of Case Address, 159
politics, Scale of Politics, 161–62
positive, current, negative, 137
postulate(s),
accomplishes change in MEST, 91
theta creates by postulates, 82
Tone Scale of, 134
valuable as it is workable, 48
potential value, equation, 41
Power Plus Release, Grade VA, 184
Power Release, Grade V, 184
preclears' secrets, Auditor's Code
on, 193
Prehavingness Scale, 142–43
pre-OT levels,
leading to personal spiritual
freedom, 174
OT I–VII, 184–85
problem,
methods of resolving, 48
must contain a lie, 91
Release, Expanded Grade I, 181
resolved through estimations of
effort, 60
processing, *see* **auditing**
propitiation, effects tolerable on
self, others, 150

Books and Tapes
by L. Ron Hubbard

To obtain any of the following materials by L. Ron Hubbard, contact the organization nearest you, or order directly from the publisher. These addresses are given at the very back of this publication. Many of these works have been translated and are available in a number of different languages.

The works are arranged in the suggested order that they be read (or listened to) within each category.

Basic Scientology Books

Scientology: The Fundamentals of Thought • Be able to resolve problems in life and raise your survival potential immensely, simply by applying the basics in this book! L. Ron Hubbard gives a new, positive outlook on life for people who like to think for themselves. He shows how the positive, good and creative life force in each individual can be enhanced to make the world a better, happier place to live. Available in bookstores everywhere.

A New Slant on Life • Have you ever asked yourself Who am I? What am I? This book of articles by L. Ron Hubbard answers these all too common questions. This is knowledge one can use every day—for a new, more confident and happier slant on life!

The Problems of Work • Work plays a big part in the game of life. Do you really enjoy your work? Are you certain of your job security? Would you like the increased personal satisfaction of doing your work well? This is the book that shows exactly how to achieve these things and more. The game of life—and within it, the game of work—can be enjoyable and rewarding.

Basic Dianetics Books

Dianetics: The Modern Science of Mental Health • Acclaimed as the most effective self-help book ever published. Dianetics technology has helped millions reach new heights of freedom and ability. Over 11,000,000 copies sold! Discover the source of mental barriers that prevent you from achieving your goals—and how to handle them!

Self Analysis • The complete do-it-yourself handbook for anyone who wants to improve his abilities and success potential. Use the simple, easy-to-learn techniques in *Self Analysis* to build self-confidence and reduce stress.

The Dynamics of Life—An Introduction to Dianetics Discoveries • Break through the barriers to your happiness. In this book, L. Ron Hubbard reveals the startling principles behind Dianetics—facts so powerful they can change forever the way you look at yourself and your potentials. Discover how you can use the powerful basic principles in this book to blast through the barriers of your mind and gain full control over your success, future and happiness.

Dianetics: The Evolution of a Science • It is estimated that we use less than ten percent of our mind's potential. What stops us from developing and using the full potential of our minds? *Dianetics: The Evolution of a Science* is L. Ron Hubbard's incredible story of how he discovered the reactive mind and how he developed the keys to unlock its secrets. Get this firsthand account of what the mind really is, and how you can release its hidden potential.

Books on the Purification Program

Purification: An Illustrated Answer to Drugs • Do toxins and drugs hold down your ability to think clearly? What is the Purification Program and how does it work? How can harmful chemical substances be gotten out of the body? Our society is ridden by abuse of drugs, alcohol and medicine that reduce one's ability to think clearly. Find out what can be done in this introduction to the Purification Program.

All About Radiation • Can the effects of radiation exposure be avoided or reduced? What exactly would happen in the event of an atomic explosion? Get the answers to these and many other questions in this illuminating book. *All About Radiation* describes observations and discoveries concerning the physical and mental effects of radiation and the possibilities for handling them. Get the real facts on the subject of radiation and its effects.

Books on Past Lives

Have You Lived Before This Life? • This is the book that sparked a flood of interest in the ancient puzzle: Does man live only one life? The answer lay in mystery, buried until L. Ron Hubbard's researches unearthed the truth. Actual case histories of people recalling past lives in auditing tell the tale.

Mission Into Time • Here is a fascinating account of a unique research expedition into both space and time, locating physical evidence of past lives in an area rich with history—the Mediterranean.

Dianetics Graduate Books

Science of Survival • If you ever wondered why people act the way they do, you'll find this book a wealth of information. It's vital to anyone who wants to understand others and improve personal relationships. *Science of Survival* is built around a re-markable chart—The Hubbard Chart of Human Evaluation. With it you can understand and predict other people's behavior and reactions and greatly increase your control over your own life. This is a valuable handbook that can make a difference between success and failure on the job and in life.

Dianetics 55! • Your success in life depends on your ability to communicate. Do you know a formula exists for communication? Learn the rules of better communication that can help you live a more fulfilling life. Here, L. Ron Hubbard deals with the fundamental principles of communication and how you can master these to achieve your goals.

Child Dianetics • Here is a revolutionary new approach to rearing children with the techniques of Dianetics technology. Find out how you can help your child achieve greater confidence, more self-reliance, improved learning rate and a happier, more loving relationship with you.

Notes on the Lectures • In the rush of excitement following the release of *Dianetics: The Modern Science of Mental Health*, L. Ron Hubbard was in demand all over the world as a speaker. This book is compiled from his fascinating lectures given right after the publication of *Dianetics: The Modern Science of Mental Health*. In them, he expands on the powerful principles of Dianetics and its application to groups.

Advanced Scientology Books

Scientology 8-8008 • Get the basic truths about your nature as a spiritual being and your relationship to the physical universe around you. Here, L. Ron Hubbard describes procedures designed to increase your abilities to heights previously only dreamed of.

Scientology 8-80 • What are the laws of life? We are all familiar with physical laws such as the law of gravity, but what laws govern life and thought? L. Ron Hubbard answers the riddles of life and its goals in the physical universe.

Scientology: A History of Man • A cold-blooded and factual account of the ancient background and history of the human race—revolutionary concepts guaranteed to intrigue you and challenge many basic assumptions about man's true power, potential and abilities.

The Phoenix Lectures • An in-depth look at the roots of Scientology religious philosophy and how it was developed is contained in this work. The influence of earlier great philosophies and religious leaders is covered in detail. This is followed by a complete discussion of the nature of existence and reality, and exactly how man interacts with his environment. An enlightening look at the infinite potentialities of man.

The Creation of Human Ability • Improve your life, and the lives of others, far beyond current expectations. Learn simple yet powerful techniques you can use to help somebody increase his ability and operate more successfully in life.

Handbook for Preclears • This personal workbook contains easily done exercises to help you improve your life and find greater happiness.

Advanced Procedure and Axioms • For the *first* time the basics of thought and the physical universe have been codified into a set of fundamental laws, signaling an entire new way to view and approach the subjects of man, the physical universe and even life itself.

Dictionaries

Basic Dictionary of Dianetics and Scientology • Compiled from the works of L. Ron Hubbard, this convenient dictionary contains the terms and expressions needed by anyone learning Dianetics and Scientology technology. And a *special bonus*—an easy-to-read Scientology Organizing Board chart that shows you whom to contact for services and information at your nearest Scientology Organization.

Dianetics and Scientology Technical Dictionary • This dictionary is your indispensable guide to the words and ideas of Scientology and Dianetics technologies—technologies which can help you increase your know-how and effectiveness in life. Over three thousand words are defined—including a new understanding of vital words like *life, love* and *happiness* as well as Scientology terms.

Modern Management Technology Defined: Hubbard Dictionary of Administration and Management • Here's a real breakthrough in the subject of administration and management! Eighty-six hundred words are defined for greater understanding of any business situation. Clear, precise Scientology definitions describe many previously baffling phenomena and bring truth, sanity and understanding to the often murky field of business management.

Basic Executive Books

How to Live Though an Executive • What is the one factor in business and commerce which, if lacking, can keep a person overworked and worried, keep labor and management at each other's throats, and make an unsafe working atmosphere? L. Ron Hubbard reveals principles based on years of research into many different types of organizations.

Introduction to Scientology Ethics • Find out how to improve conditions and reach higher states of awareness and survival in one's job, family and life. Here's a practical book to be applied in all aspects of your life. *Introduction to Scientology Ethics* explains how to live a more honest and ethical life. Here is a practical system for helping you achieve your goals.

Graduate Executive Books

Organization Executive Course • The *Organization Executive Course* volumes contain workable organizational technology never before known to man. This is not just how a Scientology organization works; this is how the operation of *any* organization, *any* activity, can be improved. A person knowing the data in these volumes fully, and applying it, could completely reverse any downtrend in a company—or even a country!

Management Series Volume 1 • Never before has such a collection of state-of-the-art management technology been available for instant use. This large volume gives you the secrets of organizing anything to flow smoothly and efficiently with increased production and viability.

Management Series Volume 2 • Here is high-tech for any business executive or manager. In this 768-page volume you get down to the basics of finance, personnel, marketing and public relations. Get powerful data to strategically plan and coordinate so you can accomplish any objective. Learn how to be a powerful, effective executive and stay one.

Reference Materials

Background and Ceremonies of the Church of Scientology • Discover the beautiful and inspiring ceremonies of the Church of Scientology, and its fascinating religious and historical background. This book contains the illuminating Creed of the

Church, church services, sermons and ceremonies, many as originally given in person by L. Ron Hubbard, Founder of Scientology.

What is Scientology? • Scientology applied religious philosophy has attracted great interest and attention since its beginning. What is Scientology philosophy? What can it accomplish —and why are so many people from all walks of life proclaiming its effectiveness? Find the answers to these questions and many others in *What is Scientology?*

Books to Help You Counsel Others

Introductory and Demonstration Processes and Assists • How can you help someone increase his enthusiasm for living? How can you improve someone's self-confidence on the job? Here are basic Scientology processes you can use to help others deal with life and living.

Volunteer Minister's Handbook • This is a big, practical how-to-do-it book to give a person the basic knowledge on how to help self and others through the rough spots in life. It consists of twenty-one sections—each one covering important situations in life, such as drug and alcohol problems, study difficulties, broken marriages, accidents and illnesses, failing businesses, difficult children, and much more. This is the basic tool with which to help someone out of troubles and bring about a happier life.

The Classic Cassettes Series

There are nearly three thousand recorded lectures by L. Ron Hubbard on the subjects of Dianetics and Scientology. What follows is a sampling of these lectures, each known and loved the world over. All of the Classic Cassettes are presented in Clear-sound state-of-the-art sound-recording technology, notable for its clarity and brilliance of reproduction.

Scientology and Effective Knowledge • Voyage to new horizons of awareness! *Scientology and Effective Knowledge* by L. Ron Hubbard can help you understand more about yourself and others. A fascinating tale of the beginnings of Dianetics and Scientology.

The Story of Dianetics and Scientology • In this lecture, L. Ron Hubbard shares with you his earliest insights into human nature and gives a compelling and often humorous account of his experiences. Spend an unforgettable time with Ron as he talks about the start of Dianetics and Scientology!

The Road to Truth • The road to truth has eluded man since the beginning of time. In this classic lecture, L. Ron Hubbard explains what this road actually is and why it is the only road one MUST travel all the way once begun. This lecture reveals the only road to higher levels of living.

My Philosophy • Three dramatic essays written by Ron— "My Philosophy," "The Aims of Scientology" and "A Description of Scientology"—come alive for you in this cassette. These powerful writings, beautifully read and set to new and inspiring music, tell you what Scientology is, what it does and what its aims are.

More advanced books and lectures are available. Contact your nearest organization or write directly to the publisher for a full catalog.

Improve Your Life with Scientology Extension Courses

Scientology books by L. Ron Hubbard give you the knowledge to achieve a happier, more successful life. Now learn to take and *use* that knowledge to gain greater control of *your* life. Enroll on a Scientology Extension Course.

Each extension course package includes a lesson booklet with easy to understand instructions and all the lessons you will need to complete it. Each course can be done in the comfort and convenience of your own home. Simply mail the completed lessons once a week to the Extension Course Supervisor at your Church of Scientology, who will review it and mail the results back to you. When you complete the course you will be sent a beautiful certificate suitable for framing.

The Fundamentals of Thought Extension Course

Here is *practical, workable* knowledge that can improve your life in today's troubled world. The *Fundamentals of Thought Extension Course* contains lessons to ensure that you fully understand the data and can use it. Under the guidance of a professional Extension Course Supervisor, you can gain far greater understanding of life as you complete each lesson by mail. Order the *Fundamentals of Thought Extension Course* today!

A New Slant on Life
Extension Course

Life does not have to remain the same. You *can* reach higher levels of knowledge, ability and freedom. Discover the two rules for happy living, the secret of success, how to avoid being a "cog in a machine," how to reach your goals and more. Do the *New Slant on Life Extension Course* and gain a refreshing new outlook on life!

The Problems of Work
Extension Course

Trying to handle a job and keep it can get to be a deadlier struggle with each working day. What are the secrets to increasing your enjoyment of work? How can you gain the personal satisfaction of doing your work well? Find the answers and apply them easily. Do *The Problems of Work Extension Course!*

Enroll on a
Scientology Home Study
Extension Course Today!

For information and enrollment and prices for these extension courses and the books they accompany, contact the Public Registrar at your nearest Church of Scientology. (A complete list of Scientology Churches and Organizations is provided at the back of this book.)

"The success level of a person *is* his communication level."

—*L. Ron Hubbard*

Your success on the job, in handling a home, in creating relationships based on *honesty* and *trust* depends on *your ability to communicate.*

The Success Through Communication Course by L. Ron Hubbard is a vital and *practical* course to help you improve communication and be more effective in life. Discover the eighteen exact, simple and powerful techniques that will show you how to:

- Get your point across and really be understood!
- Begin a conversation with anyone—even with a silent person!
- Listen effectively!
- Handle any upset in communication!
- End any conversation when you want to

  —and much more!

Learn these effective communication techniques on weekdays, evenings or weekends.

Do the *Success Through Communication Course* by L. Ron Hubbard

Start today!

Contact the Public Registrar at your nearest Church of Scientology.

(A complete list of Scientology Churches or Organizations and their addresses is provided at the back of this book.)

Get Your Free Catalog of Knowledge on How to Improve Life

L. Ron Hubbard's books and tapes increase your ability to understand yourself and others. His works give you the practical know-how you need to improve your life and the lives of your family and friends.

Many more materials by L. Ron Hubbard are available than have been covered in the pages of this book. A free catalog of these materials is available on request.

Write for your free catalog today!

Bridge Publications, Inc.
4751 Fountain Avenue
Los Angeles, California 90029

New Era Publications International, ApS
Store Kongensgade 55
1264 Copenhagen K, Denmark

For more information about Scientology or to order books and cassettes

Call: **1-800-367-8788**
in the U.S. and Canada

Is there such a thing as a hotline that doesn't believe in giving advice? What about a hotline for able individuals to help them solve their *own* problems?

"If we take a man and keep giving him advice," L. Ron Hubbard has said, "we don't necessarily wind up with a resolution of his problems. But if, on the other hand, we put him in a position where he had higher intelligence, where his reaction time was better, where he could confront life better, where he could identify the factors in his life more easily, then he's in a position where he can solve his own problems."

Call the unique new hotline and referral service with operators trained in Scientology technology. Callers find someone they can trust to talk to about a problem, and they are referred to their nearest Scientology church or organization for more information if they are interested.

You can also order books and cassettes by L. Ron Hubbard by calling this number.

Call this toll-free number
7 days a week
from 9 A.M. to 11 P.M. Pacific Standard Time.

Ensure You Have
Your Membership

You are entitled to a free 6 month membership in the International Association of Scientologists™. As a member you'll enjoy a 20% discount on all LRH™ books, tapes, films and other Bookstore items, as well as further services at your Church of Scientology®.

Additionally you'll receive IMPACT, the news-filled magazine only for International Association of Scientologists Members.

This membership will help you in your journey toward a happier, more successful life.

Join the
International Association of Scientologists
Contact the Membership Officer at your Church of Scientology now

"I am always happy to hear from my readers."

L. Ron Hubbard

These were the words of L. Ron Hubbard, who was always very interested in hearing from his friends, readers and followers. He made a point of staying in communication with everyone he came in contact with over his fifty-year career as a professional writer, and he had thousands of fans and friends that he corresponded with all over the world.

The publishers of L. Ron Hubbard's literary works wish to continue this tradition and would welcome letters and comments from you, his readers, both old and new.

Any message addressed to the Author's Affairs Director at Bridge Publications will be given prompt and full attention.

Bridge Publications, Inc.
4751 Fountain Avenue
Los Angeles, California 90029
U.S.A.

Church and Organization Address List

United States of America

Albuquerque
Church of Scientology
1210 San Pedro NE
Albuquerque, New Mexico 87110

Ann Arbor
Church of Scientology
301 North Ingalls Street
Ann Arbor, Michigan 48104

Austin
Church of Scientology
2200 Guadalupe
Austin, Texas 78705

Boston
Church of Scientology
448 Beacon Street
Boston, Massachusetts 02115

Buffalo
Church of Scientology
47 West Huron Street
Buffalo, New York 14202

Chicago
Church of Scientology
3011 North Lincoln Avenue
Chicago, Illinois 60657

Cincinnati
Church of Scientology
215 West 4th Street, 5th Floor
Cincinnati, Ohio 45202

Columbus
Church of Scientology
167 East State Street
Columbus, Ohio 43215

Dallas
Church of Scientology
Celebrity Centre Dallas
8501 Manderville Lane
Dallas, Texas 75231

Denver
Church of Scientology
375 South Navajo Street
Denver, Colorado 80223

Detroit
Church of Scientology
321 Williams Street
Royal Oak, Michigan 48067

Honolulu
Church of Scientology
1100 Alakea Street #301
Honolulu, Hawaii 96813

Kansas City
Church of Scientology
3742 Broadway, Suite 203
Kansas City, Missouri 64111

Las Vegas
Church of Scientology
846 East Sahara Avenue
Las Vegas, Nevada 89104

Las Vegas *(cont.)*
Church of Scientology
Celebrity Centre Las Vegas
1100 South 10th Street
Las Vegas, Nevada 89104

Long Island
Church of Scientology
330 Fulton Avenue
Hempstead, New York 11550

Los Angeles and vicinity
Church of Scientology
4810 Sunset Boulevard
Los Angeles, California 90027

Church of Scientology
1451 Irvine Boulevard
Tustin, California 92680

Church of Scientology
263 East Colorado Boulevard
Pasadena, California 91101

Church of Scientology
10335 Magnolia Boulevard
North Hollywood, California 91601

Church of Scientology
American Saint Hill Organization
1413 North Berendo Street
Los Angeles, California 90027

Church of Scientology
American Saint Hill Foundation
1413 North Berendo Street
Los Angeles, California 90027

Church of Scientology
Advanced Organization of
  Los Angeles
1306 North Berendo Street
Los Angeles, California 90027

Church of Scientology
Celebrity Centre International
5930 Franklin Avenue
Hollywood, California 90028

Miami
Church of Scientology
120 Giralda Avenue
Coral Gables, Florida 33134

Minneapolis
Church of Scientology
3019 Minnehaha Avenue
Minneapolis, Minnesota 55406

New Haven
Church of Scientology
909 Whalley Avenue
New Haven, Connecticut 06515

New York City
Church of Scientology
227 West 46th Street
New York City, New York 10036

Church of Scientology
Celebrity Centre New York
65 East 82nd Street
New York City, New York 10028

Orlando
Church of Scientology
710-A East Colonial Drive
Orlando, Florida 32803

Philadelphia
Church of Scientology
1315 Race Street
Philadelphia, Pennsylvania 19107

Phoenix
Church of Scientology
4450 North Central Avenue, Suite 102
Phoenix, Arizona 85012

Portland
Church of Scientology
1536 South East 11th Avenue
Portland, Oregon 97214

Church of Scientology
Celebrity Centre Portland
709 South West Salmon Street
Portland, Oregon 97205

Sacramento
Church of Scientology
825 15th Street
Sacramento, California 95814

San Diego
Church of Scientology
2409 Fourth Avenue
San Diego, California 92101

San Francisco
Church of Scientology
83 McAllister Street
San Francisco, California 94102

San Jose
Church of Scientology
3604 Stevens Creek Boulevard
San Jose, California 95117

Santa Barbara
Church of Scientology
524 State Street
Santa Barbara, California 93101

Seattle
Church of Scientology
2004 Westlake Avenue
Seattle, Washington 98121

St. Louis
Church of Scientology
9510 Page Boulevard
St. Louis, Missouri 63132

Tampa
Church of Scientology
4809 North Armenia Avenue, Suite 215
Tampa, Florida 33603

Clearwater
Church of Scientology
Flag® Service Organization
210 South Fort Harrison Avenue
Clearwater, Florida 33516

Washington, D.C.
Founding Church of Scientology
2125 "S" Street N.W.
Washington, D.C. 20008

Canada

Edmonton
Church of Scientology
10349 82nd Avenue
Edmonton, Alberta
Canada T6E 1Z9

Kitchener
Church of Scientology
8 Water Street North
Kitchener, Ontario
Canada N2H 5A5

Montreal
Church of Scientology
4489 Papineau Street
Montréal, Québec
Canada H2H 1T7

Ottawa
Church of Scientology
150 Rideau Street, 2nd Floor
Ottawa, Ontario
Canada K1N 5X6

Quebec
Church of Scientology
226 St-Joseph est
Québec, Québec
Canada G1K 3A9

Toronto
Church of Scientology
696 Yonge Street
Toronto, Ontario
Canada M4Y 2A7

Vancouver
Church of Scientology
401 West Hastings Street
Vancouver, British Columbia
Canada V6B 1L5

Winnipeg
Church of Scientology
Suite 125—388 Donald Street
Winnipeg, Manitoba
Canada R3B 2J4

United Kingdom

Birmingham
Church of Scientology
80 Hurst Street
Birmingham
England B5 4TD

Brighton
Church of Scientology
Dukes Arcade, Top Floor
Dukes Street
Brighton, Sussex
England

East Grinstead
Saint Hill Foundation
Saint Hill Manor
East Grinstead, West Sussex
England RH19 4JY

Advanced Organization Saint Hill
Saint Hill Manor
East Grinstead, West Sussex
England RH19 4JY

Edinburgh
Hubbard Academy of Personal
    Independence
20 Southbridge
Edinburgh, Scotland EH1 1LL

London
Church of Scientology
68 Tottenham Court Road
London, W1P 0BB England

Manchester
Church of Scientology
258 Deansgate
Manchester, England M3 4BG

Plymouth
Church of Scientology
41 Ebrington Street
Plymouth, Devon
England PL4 9AA

Sunderland
Church of Scientology
51 Fawcett Street
Sunderland, Tyne and Wear
England SR1 1RS

Austria

Vienna
Church of Scientology
Mariahilfer Strasse 88A/II/2
A-1070 Vienna, Austria

Belgium

Brussels
Church of Scientology
45A, Rue de l'Ecuyer
1000 Bruxelles, Belgium

Denmark

Aarhus
Church of Scientology
Guldsmedegade 17, 2
8000 Aarhus C., Denmark

Copenhagen
Church of Scientology
Store Kongensgade 55
1264 Copenhagen K, Denmark

Church of Scientology
Vesterbrogade 23 A – 25
1620 Copenhagen V, Denmark

Church of Scientology
Advanced Organization Saint Hill for
    Europe and Africa
Jernbanegade 6
1608 Copenhagen V, Denmark

France

Angers
Church of Scientology
10–12, rue Max Richard
49000 Angers, France

Clermont-Ferrand
Church of Scientology
2 Pte Rue Giscard de la Tour Fondue
63000 Clermont-Ferrand, France

Lyon
Church of Scientology
3, place des Capucins
69001 Lyon, France

Paris
Church of Scientology
65, rue de Dunkerque
75009 Paris, France

Church of Scientology
Celebrity Centre Paris
69, rue Legendre
75017 Paris, France

St. Etienne
Church of Scientology
24, rue Marengo
42000 St. Etienne, France

Germany

Berlin
Church of Scientology e.V.
Sponholzstrasse 51/52
1000 Berlin 41, Germany

Düsseldorf
Church of Scientology
Friedrichstrasse 28
4000 Düsseldorf, West Germany

Frankfurt
Church of Scientology
Darmstadter Landstr. 119–125
6000 Frankfurt/Main, West Germany

Hamburg
Church of Scientology e.V.
Steindamm 63
2000 Hamburg 1, West Germany

Church of Scientology
Celebrity Centre Hamburg
Mönckebergstrasse 5
2000 Hamburg 1
West Germany

Munich
Church of Scientology
Beichstrasse 12
D-8000 München 40, West Germany

Greece

Athens
Applied Philosophy Center of Greece
(K.E.F.E.)
Ippokratous 175B
114 72 Athens, Greece

Israel

Tel Aviv
Scientology and Dianetics College
7 Salomon Street
Tel Aviv 66023, Israel

Italy

Brescia
Church of Scientology
Dei Tre Laghi
Via Fratelli Bronzetti N. 20
25125 Brescia, Italy

Milano
Church of Scientology
Via Abetone, 10
20137 Milano, Italy

Monza
Church of Scientology
Via Cavour, 5
20052 Monza, Italy

Novara
Church of Scientology
Corso Cavallotti No. 7
28100 Novara, Italy

Nuoro
Church of Scientology
Corso Garibaldi, 108
08100 Nuoro, Italy

Padua
Church of Scientology
Via Mameli 1/5
35131 Padova, Italy

Pordenone
Church of Scientology
Via Montereale, 10/C
33170 Pordenone, Italy

Rome
Church of Scientology
Via di San Vito, 11
00185 Roma, Italy

Turin
Church of Scientology
Via Guarini, 4
10121 Torino, Italy

Verona
Church of Scientology
Vicolo Chiodo No. 4/A
37121 Verona, Italy

Netherlands

Amsterdam
Church of Scientology
Nieuwe Zijds Voorburgwal 271
1012 RL Amsterdam, Netherlands

Norway

Oslo
Church of Scientology
Storgata 9
0155 Oslo 1, Norway

Portugal

Lisbon
Instituto de Dianética
Rua Actor Taborde 39–4°
1000 Lisboa, Portugal

Spain

Barcelona
Dianética
Calle Pau Claris 85, Principal 1ª
08010 Barcelona, Spain

Madrid
Asociación Civil de Dianética
Montera 20, Piso 2
28013 Madrid, Spain

Sweden

Göteborg
Church of Scientology
Norra Hamngatan 4
S-411 14 Göteborg, Sweden

Malmö
Church of Scientology
Stortorget 27
S-211 34 Malmö, Sweden

Stockholm
Church of Scientology
Kammakargatan 46
S-111 60 Stockholm, Sweden

Switzerland

Basel
Church of Scientology
Herrengrabenweg 56
4054 Basel, Switzerland

Bern
Church of Scientology
Effingerstrasse 25
CH-3008 Bern, Switzerland

Geneva
Church of Scientology
4, rue du Léman
1201 Genève, Switzerland

Lausanne
Church of Scientology
10, rue de la Madeleine
1003 Lausanne, Switzerland

Zurich
Church of Scientology
Badenerstrasse 294
CH-8004 Zürich, Switzerland

Australia

Adelaide
Church of Scientology
24 Waymouth Street
Adelaide, South Australia 5000
Australia

Brisbane
Church of Scientology
2nd Floor, 106 Edward Street
Brisbane, Queensland 4000
Australia

Canberra
Church of Scientology
Suite 16, 108 Bunda Street
Canberra Civic
A.C.T. 2601, Australia

Melbourne
Church of Scientology
44 Russell Street
Melbourne, Victoria 3000
Australia

Perth
Church of Scientology
39-41 King Street
Perth, Western Australia 6000
Australia

Sydney
Church of Scientology
201 Castlereagh Street
Sydney, New South Wales 2000
Australia

Church of Scientology
Advanced Organization Saint Hill
Australia, New Zealand and
Oceania
19-37 Greek Street
Glebe, New South Wales 2037
Australia

Japan

Tokyo
Scientology Tokyo Organization
101 Toyomi Nishi Gotanda Heights
2-13-5 Nishi Gotanda
Shinagawa-Ku
Tokyo, Japan 141

New Zealand

Auckland
Church of Scientology
2nd Floor, 44 Queen Street
Auckland 1, New Zealand

Africa

Bulawayo
Church of Scientology
74 Abercorn Street
Bulawayo, Zimbabwe

Cape Town
Church of Scientology
5 Beckham Street
Gardens
Cape Town 8001, South Africa

Durban
Church of Scientology
57 College Lane
Durban 4001, South Africa

Harare
Church of Scientology
First Floor State Lottery Building
P.O. Box 3524
Corner Speke Avenue and
   Julius Nyerere Way
Harare, Zimbabwe

Johannesburg
Church of Scientology
Security Building, 2nd Floor
95 Commissioner Street
Johannesburg 2001, South Africa

Church of Scientology
101 Huntford Building
40 Hunter Street
Cnr. Hunter & Fortesque Roads
Yeoville 2198
Johannesburg, South Africa

Port Elizabeth
Church of Scientology
2 St. Christopher
27 Westbourne Road
Port Elizabeth 6001, South Africa

Pretoria
Church of Scientology
"Die Meent Arcade," 2nd Level,
   Shop 43b
266 Pretorius Street
Pretoria 0002, South Africa

Latin America

Colombia

Bogotá
Centro Cultural de Dianética
Carrera 19 No. 39–55
Apartado Aereo 92419
Bogotá, D.E. Colombia

Mexico

Estado de México
Instituto Tecnologico de Dianética,
   A.C.
Reforma 530, Lomas
México D.F., C.P. 11000

Guadalajara
Organización Cultural Dianética de
   Guadalajara, A.C.
Av. Lopez Mateos Nte. 329
Sector Hidalgo
Guadalajara, Jalisco, México

Mexico City
Asociación Cultural Dianética, A.C.
Hermes No. 46
Colonia Crédito Constructor
03940 México 19, D.F.

Instituto de Filosofia Aplicada, A.C.
Durango #105
Colonia Roma
06700 México D.F.

Instituto de Filosofia Aplicada, A.C.
Plaza Rio de Janeiro No. 52
Colonia Roma
06700 México D.F.

Organización, Desarrollo y
   Dianética, A.C.
Providencia 1000
Colonia Del Valle C.P.
03100 México D.F.

Centro de Dianética Polanco
Insurgentes Sur 536 1er piso
   Esq. Nogales
Colonia Roma Sur C.P.
06700 México D.F.

Venezuela

Valencia
Asociación Cultural Dianética de
   Venezuela, A.C.
Ave. 101 No. 150–23
Urbanizacion La Alegria
Apartado Postal 833
Valencia, Venezuela

To obtain any books or cassettes by L. Ron Hubbard which are not available at your local organization, contact any of the following publishers:

Bridge Publications, Inc.
4751 Fountain Avenue
Los Angeles, California 90029

Continental Publications Liaison Office
696 Yonge Street
Toronto, Ontario
Canada M4Y 2A7

New Era Publications International
    ApS
Store Kongensgade 55
1264 Copenhagen K, Denmark

Era Dinámica Editores, S.A. de C.V.
Alabama 105
Colonia Nápoles
C.P. 03810 México, D.F.

NEW ERA Publications, Ltd.
78 Holmethorpe Avenue
Redhill, Surrey RH1 2NL
United Kingdom

N.E. Publications Australia Pty. Ltd.
2 Verona Street
Paddington, New South Wales 2021
Australia

Continental Publications Pty. Ltd.
P.O. Box 27080
Benrose 2011
South Africa

NEW ERA Publications Italia Srl
Via L. G. Columella, 12
20128 Milano, Italy

NEW ERA Publications GmbH
Otto—Hahn—Strasse 25
6072 Dreieich 1, Germany

NEW ERA Publications France
111, boulevard de Magenta
75010 Paris, France

New Era Publications España, S.A.
C/De la Paz, 4/1° dcha
28012 Madrid, Spain

New Era Japan
5-4-5-803 Nishigotanda
Shinagawa-Ku
Tokyo, Japan